KEEPING CHICKENS

KEEPING CHICKENS

THE ESSENTIAL GUIDE TO ENJOYING AND GETTING THE BEST FROM CHICKENS

Jeremy Hobson and Celia Lewis

FALL
RIVER
PRESS

Fall River Press
122 Fifth Avenue
New York, NY 10011

ISBN: 978-1-4351-2381-6

Printed in China

10 9 8 7 6 5 4 3 2 1

Commissioning Editor   Mic Cady
Editor   Jennifer Fox-Proverbs
Art Editor   Prudence Rogers
Production Controller   Kelly Smith
Project Editor   Rebecca Snelling
Illustrators   Emma Sandquest and Celia Lewis
Photographers Marie O'Hara and Kim Sayer

Contents

Introduction

Just as a house without clutter and the hustle and bustle of people feels like a museum, so a plot of land without chickens can be a sterile and lonely place. A garden full of flowers might be beautiful, but think how such a scene would be transformed by the glimpse through the blooms of a handsome cockerel and his harem of hens.

Chickens quite literally add 'life' to your life, providing a source of joy and relaxation after a stressful day. They are relatively inexpensive to feed and keep, will not take up too much of your time and come in such a range of shapes and sizes that they will fit in virtually anywhere. Best of all, your hens will supply you with the ingredients for many varied meals – what more could one ask for?

There is, however, no escaping the fact that people and poultry may, in certain circumstances, coexist uneasily, although with care and forethought most of the common problems can be avoided or overcome. Chickens and bantams can live alongside neighbours, herbaceous borders and a busy lifestyle, but it is important that the right breeds are chosen to match the situation. The correct numerical balance must also be struck, and the hen-house should be positioned so as not to cause offence. A guiding hand can often help with issues such as these but, in the absence of an experienced neighbour down the road, an easily read book can be just as useful.

To answer poultry-related questions before they even arise, *Keeping Chickens* clearly explains both the theory and the practical aspects of chicken keeping. It also includes craft ideas using eggs and feathers and recipes for those lovely fresh eggs, as well as providing quirky 'I never knew that' pieces of information. Who would have thought, for instance, that the Scots Dumpy was bred with short legs to stop it wandering away from the croft, or that only white eggs were seen in the UK until the arrival of Asiatic breeds in the mid-19th century? And did you know that alektorophobia is the fear of chickens?

No matter how experienced a person may be in a certain area, he or she cannot know everything there is to know about it and will still have things to learn on a daily basis. Nowhere is this more true than when keeping chickens. This book is written by two experienced poultry breeders and authors, who hope both to introduce the delights of chicken keeping to the newcomer and to share their fascination in the hobby with those who are already seasoned campaigners.

RIGHT A pair of Barbu d'Uccle bantams make themselves at home on an unusual perch.

Understanding
Chickens

Hens are the ultimate recyclers. These omnivorous birds will eat up all your leftovers, garden weeds, lawn mowings, pests such as slugs, snails and even mice, and will turn them into beautiful fresh eggs with the addition of just a small amount of layers' mash and a handful of corn. Not only are hens useful, they also make decorative, characterful and charming pets. Aside from food and water, all they require is a house and nest-boxes, shelter from the rain and sun, and a dry dust-bath.

A Brief History of the Domesticated Fowl

The red jungle fowl (*Gallus gallus*), a native of Southeast Asia, is a tropical gallinaceous member of the pheasant family and is the direct ancestor of today's domestic chicken. First raised in captivity some 5,000 years ago in India, the domestic chicken is now kept as a source of meat and eggs all over the world. Today, there are as many as 200 different breeds, some specifically developed to produce eggs, some for meat and some entirely for their beauty.

Chickens arrived in Europe in the seventh century BC; the earliest known illustration of a hen appears on Corinthian pottery dating from that time. The Romans are credited with introducing poultry to Britain when they arrived in AD 43. Chickens were associated with many superstitions by the Romans, who also used the birds for oracles. According to the Roman orator and historian Cicero, writing in the first century BC, it was considered a good omen if a hen appeared from the left, either flying or walking along the ground. The chickens' feeding behaviour was also observed when an omen was needed: the *pullarius*, who looked after the birds, opened up their cages and gave them a special kind of food. If the chickens ate it immediately, the omen was favourable; if they flapped about or flew away, the omen was bad.

The Roman author Columella wrote a treatise on agriculture in the first century AD, and gave advice on breeding and keeping chickens. He considered 200 birds the ideal sized flock for one person to supervise. Columella suggested that white chickens should be avoided as they were easily caught by birds of prey, and that coops should lie adjacent to the kitchen as smoke from fires was beneficial to their health.

Until the mid-19th century, chickens in Britain roamed free around farms and cottage gardens, foraging for themselves and laying their eggs wherever they pleased – so they had to be hunted for. But following the arrival of Asiatic breeds such as the Cochin, with their novel brown eggs, interest in chicken keeping took off and enthusiasts started confining their hens to hen-houses with attached runs. The Victorians' passion for poultry, combined with the interests of the cock-fighting fraternity (see below), led to the development of new breeds and, eventually, to the establishment of poultry clubs and exhibitions.

Cock-fighting

Interest in cock-fighting was partly responsible for the encouragement of poultry breeding in Britain, in particular the development of the Old English Game fowl. The sport originated in China and was particularly cruel – the cockerels were specially bred to be aggressive and had artificial razor-sharp points known as cockspurs fitted to their legs. The birds pecked and maimed each other with their spurs until one died, although the victor often subsequently suffered the same fate as a result of injuries. The fights were popular with spectators, who wagered large sums on the outcome. The sport was made illegal in the UK in 1849, but is still practised in Asia and in some European countries, as well as in the state of New Mexico (though it is banned elsewhere in the USA).

RIGHT Looking after the chickens was traditionally considered to be the responsibility of the farmer's wife.

Chickens in Religion

Chickens feature in many religions. In India, the cockerel is an emblem of Karthikeya, son of Lord Shiva, the Hindu god of destruction, while Hindus in Indonesia use chickens in their cremation rites. Throughout the ceremony a chicken is tethered by its leg to ensure that any evil spirits enter it rather than any family members present. After the ceremony, the chicken is taken home to resume its normal life.

•

The ancient Greeks believed that cockerels were so brave that even lions were afraid of them, and they are found as attributes of the gods Ares, Heracles and Athena. In the ancient Persian cult of Mithras, the cock bird was a symbol of the divine light and a guardian against evil.

•

In the Bible, Jesus prophesied his betrayal by Peter: 'And he said, I tell thee, Peter, the cock shall not crow this day, before that thou shalt thrice deny that thou knowest me' (Luke 22:34). As a result, the cock became a symbol of both vigilance and betrayal in Christian societies.

single comb

rose comb

v-shaped comb

cushion comb

pea comb

buttercup comb

Combs, wattles and ear lobes

One of the most distinctive features of a chicken is its comb, which, with its wattles (fleshy appendages under the beak), functions as its cooling system. Birds cannot sweat, so the chicken cools itself by circulating blood through its comb and wattles, from which body heat radiates.

There are several types of comb, the most common of which is the single comb. This has a number of serrations and stands upright on the head, although in some breeds with very large single combs the back part tends to droop to one side. In contrast, the rose comb is low and broad, lacks points and tapers off into a 'spike' at the back. There are also V-shaped combs,

walnut or cushion combs, pea combs and buttercup combs.

Surprisingly, ear-lobe colour governs egg colour: generally, if the hen has white ear lobes she will lay white-shelled eggs, whereas red ear lobes indicate brown eggs. One exception to this rule is the Araucana, which has red ear lobes but lays blue- or green-shelled eggs.

Points of a Fowl

The different breeds of poultry vary widely in appearance, colouring and feather formation, but all share the basic elements of external anatomy indicated here.

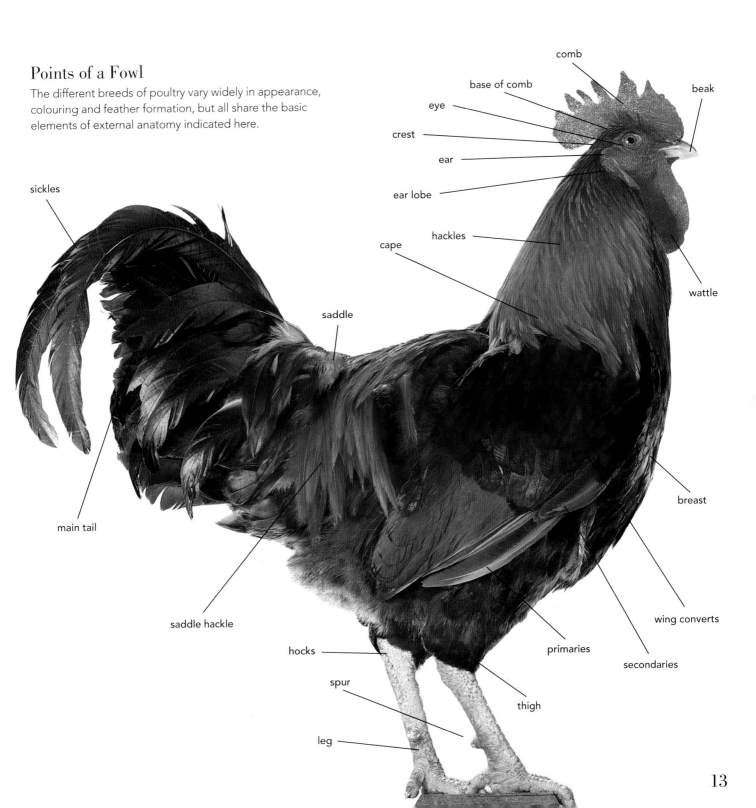

comb

base of comb

eye

beak

crest

ear

ear lobe

wattle

sickles

hackles

cape

saddle

breast

main tail

saddle hackle

wing converts

hocks

primaries

secondaries

spur

thigh

leg

13

barred

laced

spangled

pencilled

Feathers

Chicken feathers come in many colours and patterns, and provide both insulation and waterproofing. The condition of a bird's feathers is maintained through preening, which takes up a large proportion of its day and involves dust-bathing and applying oil from a gland at the base of the tail. From a zoological point of view, feathers are composed of keratin, like hair and horn, and correspond to the scales of a fish. And like scales, they overlap one another.

Poultry breeds are categorized as hard- or soft-feathered: the former are those originally bred for cock-fighting, which have smooth, close-fitting plumage. Not all birds have the same amount of feathering – some breeds have feathers right down their legs and may also have feather beards and crests.

The hackle and saddle feathers of cock birds can be distinguished from those of hens in that they tend to be pointed and shiny. The crest feathers of cock birds are the same shape as its hackles, while in hens they are shorter and broader. Cocks also have sickles, which are the long, curved feathers on either side of the tail.

Distinctive feather patterns can be used to identify the many varieties of chicken:
• **Barred** feathers have alternate transverse markings in two distinct colours.
• **Frizzled** feathers curl and curve outwards and forwards in a random manner (in the UK the Frizzle is a recognized breed – see page 41).
• **Laced** feathers have a border of a contrasting colour all around the edge.
• **Mottled** feathers have a variable percentage of black feathers tipped with white.
• **Spangled** feathers have a distinct marking of a contrasting colour, usually in a V shape at their tip.
• **Pencilled** feathers include several types of lines or markings, although most commonly they have narrow concentric linear markings following the contours of the edges.

The Pecking Order

Chickens are gregarious birds that live together as a flock, and the harmony of the group is maintained by the observation of a hierarchy, termed the pecking order, which governs where each chicken stands within the flock.

The pecking order starts with the 'top bird' and extends down to the youngest and weakest, which survive as best they can. The top bird is usually an old hen, although sometimes it is the most aggressive bird, and the rest of the flock will defer to her, often giving way at the food container.

When new birds are introduced to an established flock there are always problems because of the upset to the pecking order. A hen that spots a newcomer will utter a single warning croak, alerting the rest of the flock. If the birds were living in the wild the newcomers would be seen off, but because this is not possible in a run they may be bullied unmercifully until they are eventually accepted. One of the points in favour of keeping a cockerel is that he will stop the older members of the flock bullying the junior hens. To help protect new birds from becoming henpecked in this way, introduce them at night and never one at a time.

Without an established flock to show them what to do, new birds can be remarkably stupid about knowing that they should go into their house at night and roost on the perches provided, often preferring instead to fly up into trees or to teeter on the hen-house roof. When you buy new stock, it is a good idea to make sure that all the birds are perching happily for the first few nights; if they are not, lift them on to their perches until they learn to do this themselves.

Interesting Facts

Chickens are probably the most widespread of all domestic animals. There are approximately 29 million chickens in Britain, 271 million in the European Union and 400 million in the USA.

•

A chicken has a body temperature of 39–39.5°C (102–103°F).

•

A chicken's heart beats at the rate of 280–315 times a minute.

•

The average lifespan of a chicken is 5–7 years, although 20 years is not unknown.

•

In 1925, the average chicken laid 100 eggs a year; in 1979, a White Leghorn set the world record by laying 371 eggs in 365 days.

•

Alektorophobia is the fear of chickens.

•

Incubation starts when the egg reaches a temperature of 30°C (86°F).

•

The largest chicken egg ever recorded was laid by a Black Minorca in 1896. It weighed 340g (12oz), had a circumference of 23cm (9in) and contained five yolks.

•

The heaviest chicken on record weighed in at 10.5kg (23lb 3oz).

What to Consider

When deciding on species and systems of management, you need first to be clear about your aims. Ask yourself whether you are interested in keeping chickens for profit or self-sufficiency, or whether you want to keep them purely for the pleasure of doing so. You also need to ascertain how much time and space you have at your disposal. Little of either will not necessarily preclude you from keeping a small pen of bantams, but it will certainly remove large, feather-legged and potentially more demanding varieties from the equation.

Space

The theory behind keeping free-range poultry is wonderful but the practice is not always quite so simple. While many people's ideal is to have chickens scratching at the back door, picking at scraps and living a contented life, in reality things can be very different.

Although free-ranging poultry will eradicate insect pests and slugs in the garden, some of their habits are less welcome. Chickens and bantams love nothing more than a good dust-bath to help rid themselves of parasites, and consider a well-prepared seedbed ideal for the purpose. And to their mind, bark mulch that has been carefully placed around plants is scratching heaven. For these reasons alone, you may prefer to keep your chickens confined to a run. A run will also prevent your hens from laying in the shrubbery (see page 21) and, if well constructed, will protect them from neighbourhood dogs and any predators.

The amount of space needed in the run depends on whether your chickens can be given some free range, but generally a run should be as big as is practicable. In the interests of hygiene, two runs can be advantageous – one in use and the other 'resting' – although this does, of course, double the area needed. For more on the amount of space needed for a house and run, see Housing & Cleaning, page 64.

LEFT A contented hen roams around her patch.
ABOVE RIGHT Young children take special delight in being able to get close to fluffy, newly hatched chicks.

Children and Pets

While chickens make excellent pets for children, some breeds are known to be more aggressive or flighty than others. It may therefore be sensible, especially if you have toddlers, to avoid keeping cock birds of these breeds. Instead, opt for bantams, whose smaller size is also more likely to appeal to youngsters.

If you already have other pets, you should consider how they are likely to react to the arrival of a flock of chickens in their territory. Most cats generally get on very well with hens, but the behaviour of dogs varies according to temperament.

Most dogs will accept the flock as part of the family and show no interest in the birds, but others may attack and kill them – this is especially true with some types of bantam, which seem to have a more gamey smell. Rabbits and guinea pigs will live happily near hens but should not be put in with a flock that is fenced in a small run. Hens can be bullies and tend to peck defenceless creatures out of either curiosity or boredom. Hens and ponies are an excellent mix – ponies will enjoy the company of the birds and the hens will scratch around, eating up all the dropped food and hay seed.

Young Chicken Keepers

Keeping chickens is an excellent hobby for children, teaching them responsibility through feeding and general care, and also about food production and biology. And as hens lay eggs, they can learn about budgeting and accounts, as well as how to cook the end product.

To further children's interest in keeping birds, the Poultry Club of Great Britain organizes the Junior Certificate of Proficiency in Poultry Husbandry. This examination can be taken by children aged under 16, is free and is open to both members and non-members of the club. The syllabus is designed to establish a basic knowledge of stockmanship and poultry husbandry.

The Poultry Club also runs the annual Junior Fancier of the Year Award at the National Championship Show, but to qualify for this a youngster must first have won a Champion Juvenile award at one of that year's major regional shows. The Junior Fancier of the Year is judged with special regard to the youngster's knowledge and handling competence, as well as the quality of his or her exhibit. (For contact details of the Poultry Club of Great Britain, see the box on page 59.)

Chickens & the Garden

If you want to keep free-range chickens but at the same time would like to maintain a reasonably tidy garden, there are several tricks you can employ:

•

Choose bantams with feathered legs such as Pekins, as these don't, or can't, scratch up the grass on your lawn quite as much as other breeds.

•

Lay chicken wire flat on your herbaceous or annual beds in winter. The plants will grow up through the wire but the hens won't be able to scratch them up.

•

If dust-bathing in your beds becomes a problem, you could try tempting your birds away from them with an irresistible box of dry sand or peat. If you place it in a sunny position they may prefer it to the flower-beds.

•

If your hens take to laying outside rather than in the cosy nest-boxes you have provided, do not let them out of their run until mid-morning, by which time most should have finished laying. Some birds may, however, wait to visit their favourite spot, in which case you will have to spy on them, as they won't go near it if they know they are being watched.

•

Fertilize your plants with the manure your chickens produce – around 100g (4oz) per bird per day. It is high in nitrogen, which keeps foliage green and makes an excellent lawn feed when diluted in water. However, as it is high in ammonia it will burn plants if applied direct to beds. Instead, add it to your compost to allow it to break down first – it will also help to heat the heap and aid rotting.

ABOVE Chickens have distinct personalities, and watching their activities while they are roaming around outside the hen-house will help you get to know them better.

Daily Routine

Although chickens and bantams are not time-consuming to look after, they do appreciate a routine and like to be let out of their house and fed at regular times. Keeping to a daily pattern is important, so before you decide to make any purchases it is vital that you consider how you will carry out the apparently simple tasks of shutting the chickens up at night and letting them out in the morning.

In the winter months in more northerly latitudes, many people leave for work in the dark and, therefore, before the birds come down off the roost. Will there be anyone at home to let your chickens out once daybreak comes? And, if so, can you rely on them not to forget this simple chore? In the middle of summer, there may be problems at the other end of the day, as your chickens may still be scratching around when you are ready for bed. If the birds are kept in a secure pen this may not be a problem, but if they are free range there is a strong possibility that they will be taken by a nocturnal predator.

Ideally, chickens should be fed little and often. In a busy household, however, this is not always practical, so feeding morning and evening is the best option. Don't be tempted to leave out too much food: not only is this wasteful, pellets or mash can go sour if left in damp conditions and this practice will certainly encourage vermin. If food and water are given ad lib in the hen-house, the floor covering will get scratched into the feed and water will be spilt, increasing the likelihood of fungal disease.

Other parts of the daily routine include scraping the previous night's faeces from the droppings board, checking that no eggs have been broken in the nest-boxes and changing damp litter around any indoor drinking vessels. In the winter, drinkers need to be kept free of ice. (For more information on cleaning and maintenance routines, see Housing & Cleaning, page 64.)

Although none of these chores takes too long, there is no point in choosing to keep chickens if you cannot spend some time watching and enjoying their antics. In addition to providing relaxation at the end of a busy day, time spent leaning on the gate is essential in order to keep a check on your birds' well-being.

When You Go Away

When you are starting out on the exciting adventure of keeping chickens, bear in mind that you will need other people's assistance when you go away. If you live among like-minded neighbours, it is not too onerous a task for one of them to pop round each morning and evening to feed and water your birds. However, if you live down a lonely track out in the country, finding someone to take on the job may not be so simple.

Equally, a small flock of birds is not likely to cause too much bother for anyone taking over their care, but if you have several different breeding pens, incubators and rearing cages it is probably too great a responsibility for a neighbour or family friend. If you only ever have one annual holiday, you can arrange this at the least busy time in your poultry year, but if you go away regularly the size and demands of your flock should reflect this.

On this subject, also plan the pen and poultry shed layout with others in mind – a gate that falls off its hinges and traps your ankle every time you go through it might not bother you, but you can be sure that outside helpers will be a little less enthusiastic the next time you call on their assistance. You could also consider setting up an automatic watering system. There are several of these on the market that are inexpensive and easy to install, and they will save both you and your stand-ins some time. Commercially produced automatic pop-holes are also available, although if you are creative it is easy enough to design and build one yourself that is raised and lowered by the use of a small motor and timer. However, if you do install such a device you will still need someone to check that the system hasn't failed and that the birds haven't been locked in all day or, worse still, locked out at night.

Cost

Aside from the birds themselves, the initial costs of keeping chickens are those of the capital equipment – housing, wire netting, fence posts, feeders and drinkers. If you intend breeding more than the odd clutch of eggs (which can normally be done very successfully when one of the hens becomes broody), you might also consider the acquisition of a small incubator and artificial brooder.

Look after it well and there is no reason why such equipment should not remain sound and serviceable for a good 20 years or more, so the initial outlay is minimal when broken down over such a time period. When it comes to choosing equipment, the less expensive alternatives may not last quite so long, but it is worth weighing up all the options: for example, galvanized-metal drinkers and feeders are expensive but will outlive the less costly plastic ones; on the other hand, plastic is easier to keep clean.

Prices of stock will vary depending on whether you choose commercial hybrids or pure breeds, the latter usually being the more expensive. Point-of-lay stock (see Where & When to Get Your Chickens, page 56) will also cost more than youngsters that need bringing on, although you do need to take into account the extra time and food required to raise young birds to maturity. If you simply want an inexpensive source of eggs, see if you can buy layers from an intensive farm. These birds are kept by the farms for their first laying season only and so have many more years of egg-laying ahead of them.

Provided that you maintain a reasonable common-sense attitude towards the question of hygiene, it is unlikely that your flock will encounter any serious disease problems that might require the services of a veterinary surgeon. That said, there is always the faint possibility that some expensive vet's bills could be encountered at some point.

The daily running costs of keeping chickens are low, and the purchase of pelleted feeds, cereals, grit, vitamins and floor litter will generally amount to very little. You may want to have electric lighting in the hen-house for the winter months or power points from which to run an incubator, so remember to factor in the initial expense of installing these as well as the additional running costs on your electricity bill.

Some of the costs of keeping chickens can be offset by selling eggs, chicks and surplus birds, and, if you are artistic, even chicken-inspired craftwork. In reality, however, unless you keep sufficient numbers of birds to supply your customers with eggs all year round, chicken keeping can only ever be a hobby rather than a viable business venture. Never lose sight of the fact that it is almost always less expensive to buy eggs from your local supermarket. For most people, however, the excitement and appeal of collecting their own new-laid eggs from a sweet-smelling, hay-filled nest-box more than makes up for this.

By-Laws and Neighbours

Before you embark on keeping chickens, check whether any local authority or other regulations are in force that prohibit the practice in your area. If this is the case, either accept that your project is doomed to failure or consider moving house!

It is also important to explain your plans to any immediate neighbours in order to keep on the right side of them. If you do not, you might find yourself involved in a neighbourhood quarrel or even a court case that no amount of eggs offered as a sweetener will rectify.

From an environmental health point of view, rats and other vermin must be kept under control by the use of traps or poison. It is far better to take such preventative steps from the outset rather than wait until any complaints are officially registered; if this happens, you may be legally forced to get rid of your stock, and if you fail to do so you are quite likely to be prosecuted. Likewise, the owners of a loudly crowing cockerel could find themselves subject to a noise abatement order. Remember that you do not need to keep a cock bird with your flock unless you intend to breed from it, and that hens will lay just as well in the absence of a male; in fact, in some instances a cock bird can actually be a deterrent to laying (see page 28).

Depending on the size of your intended set-up, it may be necessary to obtain local authority planning permission if you want to construct a combined chicken shed, veranda and food store or even showing/isolation pens. In most cases it all comes down to overall size, whether or not the new building will be attached to an existing one, and its proximity to any neighbour's boundary. Finally, any fencing around your property must be good enough to prevent your birds wandering off your land. In most countries there is a legal requirement for you to protect other people's property from your livestock.

RIGHT Young chicks need to be kept safe from the unwanted attentions of other family pets.

Keeping Cock Birds

Technically, a cockerel is a male bird before it reaches its first adult moult (this usually takes place at around the age of 18 months), after which it becomes known as a cock. Generally, however, the term cockerel is taken to denote a young male that is under 12 months of age. Traditionally, the cock bird holds a time-honoured place in a small flock, protecting his hens, announcing the new day and helping to produce the next generation. But apart from the fact that a cock bird is necessary for breeding purposes and that he looks wonderfully colourful as he struts his stuff, is there any real reason to keep one?

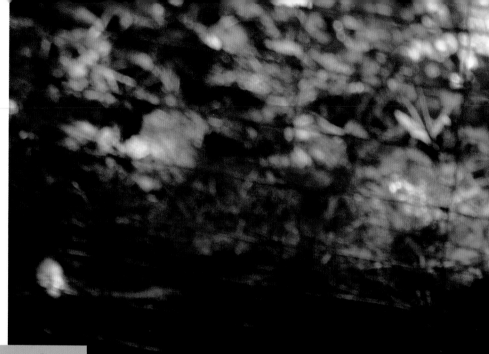

Choosing a Pet Cock Bird

The cockerels of some breeds are more aggressive than others, so it may be wise to avoid these if you have young children. Generally, the males of the heavier breeds such as Maran, New Hampshire Red, Orpington, Plymouth Rock, Rhode Island Red and Sussex are calm, placid and friendly. While the extremely heavy breeds – such as Brahma and Cochin – also make excellent pets, they may be too big for children who want to carry them around. In this case, it may be worth considering bantam varieties if these exist.

Although they were originally bred for fighting, most of the game cocks are actually extremely placid and friendly towards people, although less so towards other birds and animals. Faverolles, Silkies and Wyandottes are also all known to be non-aggressive towards people, including children.

RIGHT A Cream Legbar cockerel: this auto-sexing breed produces eggs with blue-green shells.

Why Have a Cock Bird?

Many people believe that hens will not lay without a cock bird or that they need one to watch over them, but this is untrue. In the absence of a cock, hens will find their own pecking order, or hierarchy, with one of the more dominant birds taking on the male's role. There is, however, no doubt that a cock bird enhances the pleasure of keeping chickens, even in situations where there is no real practical reason to have one. After all, there is no scene more pleasant than that of an elegant-looking male busily scratching around and drawing his hens' attention to an interesting titbit, then standing proudly over them while they peck excitedly at the treasures he has found.

While a cock bird may look magnificent, on the down side he will lay no eggs, will disturb your neighbours with his early morning crowing and will eat a lot of food. More seriously, egg production can even go down if hens are stressed and injured by a cock bird's attentions during mating. In particular, his spurs and claws can damage their backs and he will also pull out their head feathers while trying to hold on. The more submissive the hen, the more likely it is that the male bird will try to mate with her, and so the more she will suffer from broken feathers and scratches as a consequence of his attentions.

Overcoming Problems

Some breeds of chicken are known to be more aggressive than others, so if you decide to keep any of these it will pay not to include a cock bird in the flock unless absolutely necessary. Certain breeds, such as the Ko-Shamo, also crow less loudly than others, something that might further influence your initial choice of which type to purchase. Although it is actually impossible to stop a cock from crowing altogether, some preventative measures for this and other problems will work with varying degrees of success.

'Curing' Crowing

Most complaints against cock birds come down to the fact that they crow at dawn, which can be particularly annoying in the summer months when it gets light very early. A cock needs to raise his head before he can crow, something he will be less inclined to do if the hen-house is a small coop and the perch is fixed high. However, this method of prevention works only when he is actually on the perch and so will simply delay crowing until he is let out rather than curing it altogether.

It is sometimes possible to prevent a cock from crowing too early by creating some sort of shutter system, whereby the chicken house is made totally dark. If you do try this method, it is essential to make sure that there is still adequate ventilation and fresh air for all the roosting birds. Another option, but one that is time-consuming on a daily basis, is to remove the cockerel each evening and house him in a box or specially constructed cage at the rear of a garden shed, garage or similar outbuilding well away from your house and those of your neighbours.

Preventing Damage to the Hens

The simplest way to prevent a cock injuring hens is to ensure that the flock is large enough for the cock to divide his attentions between all the hens rather than concentrating on just a few. In a breeding pen where only one cock and three or four hens of one variety are required, introduce a few extra hens, preferably ones that lay a different coloured egg so that the correct eggs can be identified for hatching. A

ratio of one cock to ten hens seems to alleviate the problem in most breeds, but it is interesting to note that sometimes one or two of the hens are not fertile because they are not compatible with that particular cock bird. Another option would be to purchase lightweight canvas saddles, which are attached to the hens' backs to protect them from damage during mating.

It is also possible to trim the spurs of a cock bird, either with a strong pair of clippers normally used for trimming the claws of dogs, or by the use of a hot blade that cauterizes as it cuts (bleeding is always a possibility when an inexperienced person attempts the former method). A traditional method of removing spurs uses a potato that has been baked in an oven for an hour and then cut in half. Protect the cockerel's legs and feet by wrapping them in a towel or rolled sheets of kitchen paper, then push each half of the potato on to a spur. Hold the potato halves in place for five minutes with the aid of a thick gardening glove, then remove the potatoes. The spurs should then come away with a firm but gentle push and a quick twist.

Selecting a Breeding Cock

The cock bird is the most important member of the breeding pen, and if his background is doubtful many of his faults will be transferred to his offspring. Therefore, if he is to have any hope of producing good chicks, he must himself have come from quality breeding stock. He should be of the type outlined in the breed standards, and he should be well muscled and firm to handle. His eye colour should be bold and even, and should surround a perfectly black pupil. The comb should also conform to the breed requirements and his legs should be clean and strong – without sound legs and feet, he will find it very difficult to mount and mate with his hens. Age is also an important factor: while a cockerel is sexually mature from around six months, it is better to choose a bird that was bred in the previous spring or early summer.

Double Mating

The method of breeding known as double mating requires two distinct strains of birds: one to produce exhibition males

(this strain is called cock breeders) and the other for exhibition females (pullet breeders). It is usually carried out to create a particular plumage type or colour, good examples being the Partridge Wyandotte and Pencilled Hamburg.

In the Partridge Wyandotte, the breed standards require males to have a solid black breast, something that is achieved by crossing indistinctly marked hens with exhibition-standard cock birds. The female chicks produced in this line are not suitable for showing. For their part, exhibition pullets require pencilling, a marking that is produced by crossing cock birds that display a mixture of brown and black in their breast plumage with exhibition-standard hens. Like the females produced from the cock-breeding strain, the male offspring of pullet breeders are not suitable for exhibition.

If you do decide to keep a breed that requires two strains, your selection of cock birds must obviously reflect this (see Breeding Chickens, page 102). In addition, you will need at least two runs so that the separate lines can be kept apart.

Choosing the Breed

Chickens are such characters and are so attractive that it is easy to fall in love with each and every breed. However, before making a final decision on what type best suits you, it is as well to spend time at some of the shows and exhibitions, taking notes and talking to breeders. Part of the pleasure of keeping chickens is knowing something about the various breeds and how to distinguish between them.

Pure Breeds and Hybrids

There are countless pure breeds of large fowl to choose from. Many of the old breeds have excellent qualities both as meat producers and as egg layers, especially when they are kept in non-intensive management systems. Such birds may cost more initially, but there is the pleasure of knowing that you are ensuring the future welfare of a recognized breed. As the chicken-keeping bug takes over your life – and it surely will – you might also consider showing your stock, an option that would not be possible if you opted for hybrids.

A hybrid is the result of a cross between two or more breeds. Such a bird will not breed true and reproduce chicks in its own likeness; instead, for more of the same type you will have to go back to the original parent stock and breed from them again. You could, of course, keep an ever-changing flock of hybrid birds by periodically introducing totally unrelated cock birds and breeding them with your nucleus of hens. However, if you do this, the desirable points so obvious in the original stock may well be diluted in the subsequent generations. On the plus side, hybrid birds tend to be noticeably more vigorous and productive than pure breeds, which is why the vast majority of modern commercial birds are hybrid stock.

Bantams

The small breeds known as bantams are the obvious choice where space is limited. It is possible to find most of the large breeds of poultry in a bantamized version, although some birds in this category are 'true' bantams, which means that they do not have a larger counterpart. True bantams are kept mainly for ornamental or exhibition purposes, or as pets, and will not provide you with a year-round supply of breakfast eggs.

While some of the true bantams are compact, clean-legged little birds that are easy to keep, others may need special care owing to their beards, crests, long sweeping tails or heavily feathered legs and feet. Of course, the same problems could arise when choosing some of the bantamized types of large fowl, but as there are many more easily manageable breeds to choose from in this category, it should be possible to find one that suits your individual circumstances perfectly.

Meat, Eggs or Exhibition?

Many of the heavy breeds of poultry were originally produced to fulfil two purposes: any surplus cockerels were fattened for the table, while the pullets were kept for their egg-laying abilities (and at the end of their productive years they were also killed and eaten). Most of the dual-purpose breeds remain a good choice for the beginner, as they make excellent pets and become quite tame with careful daily handling. They are also usually good-looking birds and are less flighty than many of the egg-laying breeds, and so require less in the way of high fencing. Any of the pure breeds can also be exhibited in poultry shows.

Table Breeds

Modern-day broilers are usually hybrids based on the White Rock and Cornish Game, and score over the pure breeds for their ratio of meat to bone, their speed of growth and their ultimate weight. Despite this, it is generally thought that the meat of these hybrids is bland and tasteless in comparison to more traditional pure types of table bird such as the Crève-coeur and Indian Game.

As they are large and heavy in stature, any of the table breeds can be kept with the minimum amount of fencing. In addition, their calm, placid nature makes them ideal pets and companions, and means that they are gentle towards each other. Despite being developed for meat, some breeds also lay surprisingly well and have a natural tendency towards going broody, which is a good thing should you consider breeding from your own stock. One point to bear in mind, however, is that they tend to become overweight if they are not allowed free range and/or are fed a diet too high in calories.

Layers

Most of the commercial hybrid layers originated from the Rhode Island Red and White Leghorn, as both of these breeds are known to produce a constant supply of eggs. To produce an auto-sexing breed, the Legbar was developed by crossing a Brown Leghorn with a Barred Rock. The sex of day-old Legbar chicks is easily seen, as the females have clear barring on the head and back, while the cockerels have poorly defined barring. The cross between a Rhode Island Red cockerel and a Light Sussex hen also produces auto-sexed chicks – day-old pullets are brown and cockerels are silver. These hybrid strains were popular in the 1940s, and although they are now very much in decline, they would be a wonderful challenge for a novice enthusiast should an egg-layer be all that is required.

Pure layer breeds are often classified as 'light', and as such they tend towards flightiness and generally never become quite as tame as other breeds. This is important to consider when there are children around or if you want a pet bird. Because these birds are flighty, it may be necessary to build taller sides to their run or to top it with nylon netting. Another alternative would be to clip one wing of each bird, although if you do you will not be able to exhibit them until after their next moult.

Showing

For some poultry keepers, exhibiting birds is the only reason for choosing a particular breed. Showing is not only fun but is also an excellent way of keeping in regular contact with other chicken fanciers and with breeders of good-quality birds.

It is best to start with small local shows, which are organized by poultry societies or bantam clubs. As you gain experience (and provided that your birds are good enough), it may eventually be worth considering regional or annual shows, where there may be several thousand birds competing under one roof. The main period for showing is in winter, because chicks that hatch in early spring are fully grown in mid-autumn and by then yearling birds will have recently acquired their new plumage.

Entry forms and schedules are normally available a couple of months before the show date. The schedule will contain all you need to know: the date and location of the show, the cost of entry, the types of classes and, most importantly, the closing date for entries. It should also tell you when you can pen your birds and the earliest hour that you will be allowed to take them home. It is important that you read the schedule carefully and enter your birds in the correct classes. Birds that are going to be exhibited need to be chosen

with care and prepared thoroughly before the event. They must conform to breed standards and also need to be 'trained' to show themselves to their best advantage.

How Many?

When deciding on the number of birds to purchase, you first need to be clear about your expectations. Do you want a regular turn-around of table birds or a year-round supply of eggs? Do you want to rear chicks? Is it your intention to produce exhibition birds?

Generally speaking, six hens of a breed known for its laying capabilities will provide sufficient eggs for a family of four. At certain times of the year, such as in the late summer/early autumn when the birds are in moult, egg production will drop, but it shouldn't cease altogether. Hens tend to lay more sporadically in the winter months because of the reduced daylight hours, but if they are kept in draught-proof surroundings in a sunny location and are adequately fed, they should be less affected by the shorter days. If egg production does tail off, set up a light bulb in the hen-house and switch it on for a while at dawn or dusk to extend the 'daylight' hours.

AMROCK

The Amrock originates from America and is a dual-purpose utility bird that was developed from the Plymouth Rock (see page 50). Nowadays, it is kept mainly by fanciers, who favour it for the fact that it can become very tame with careful handling. It is less likely to go broody than some of the other heavy breeds and it also lays a good quantity of large brown eggs.

The Amrock is a handsome bird that is deep and rounded in shape. Its colouring is similar to that of the Plymouth Rock and Maran, but the barred markings are unique in that the cock bird has white and black bars of equal width, while on the hen the black bars are twice as broad as the white ones. The comb is single, and good specimens have yellow legs, although those of the hens will fade to almost white during periods of intense laying.

ANCONA

Anconas are an ideal beginner's bird but can have a tendency towards flightiness. It was once thought that they were derived from the Mottled Leghorn and were, therefore, a member of the Leghorn family rather than a separate breed, but this is now known to be untrue. The Ancona originated in Italy and was introduced into Britain in 1851, from where it was then exported to other countries, including the United States.

Most commonly black or, more accurately, beetle-green in colour, each feather of an Ancona has a white, V-shaped edge to its tip. Chocolate- and blue-coloured birds also occur and similarly have white tips to every feather. Interestingly, the white tips tend to become bigger after each moult. The comb is usually single, but rose-comb varieties are sometimes seen. Anconas are classified as light and soft-feathered, and are prolific layers of white eggs.

ANDALUSIAN

This soft-feathered Mediterranean breed originated in Spain – the bird seen in the UK today was developed from black and white stock imported from there in the mid-1800s. By the mid-20th century the Andalusian had become rare, but it seems to have regained its popularity and it is now possible to see specimens at shows in many countries. In the US, it is known as the Andalusian Blue.

Andalusians display colour variations. Each blue feather is surrounded by black lacing, apart from the sickle feathers of the male and the neck hackles of the female, both of which are black. The comb is single and of medium size: the cock bird's is well serrated and erect, while that of the female normally flops over to one side. The hen is a good layer of white eggs but, like the Ancona, can be nervy and flighty. The Andalusian is classified as a light breed and is soft-feathered.

ARAUCANA

In most countries, two types of Araucana are seen: tailed and rumpless. The rumpless variety is more akin to the original breed first kept many years ago by the Arauca Indians of Chile, but today it is the slightly rarer of the two. A further defining feature of the breed is the tufts of feathers sticking out of the birds' ears; known as ear-rings or ear-tufts, ideally these should slant backwards. The tailed variety also has feathered head crests and beards, and both types have a pea comb that is irregular in shape.

Classified as light and soft-feathered, the breed contains at least 11 colour varieties. The most popular of these is lavender, but it also comes in partridge, silver-blue partridge, yellow partridge, fawn, wheaten, white, black and cuckoo. Another unusual characteristic of the breed is the fact that the hens lay blue/green eggs (US standards describe the colour as turquoise). Like the Andalusian, the Araucana is a good layer and, being hardy, makes an interesting choice for the novice chicken keeper.

AUSTRALORP

The name of this breed is an abbreviation of 'Australian Black Orpington'. It resulted from stock birds imported to the UK from Australia around the 1920s being crossed with the Black Orpington, which was developed by William Cook in the late 1800s. The Australorp can, therefore, be said to be both British and Australian in origin. This soft-feathered bird is heavy and is traditionally black in colour, although white- and blue-laced variations do occur. The comb is single, serrated and of medium size, and the eggs are tinted towards brown in colour.

Australorps are easy to keep and become very tame, so they make good pets for children. Unlike some other breeds, they are also non-aggressive towards one another – even young cockerels being reared as part of a breeding programme can normally be kept together without mishap.

BARNEVELDER

Imported from the Netherlands to the UK and the US in the early 1920s, the Barnevelder possesses a single comb and is classified as soft-feathered and heavy. It is thought that the breed has Cochin, Langshan and Brahma genes in its make-up, a mixture that has resulted in a large range of colours. Nowadays, however, the only colours that are accepted as being in accordance with most countries' breed standards are black, white, double-laced and blue double-laced, although in Germany blue and brown are also permitted on the show bench.

Any of the colour varieties would make a good choice for the first-time chicken fancier, as they are all easy to keep – either free range or in a grass run – and, like the Australorp, have an easygoing and placid temperament. In addition, the hens lay a good number of dark brown eggs through the year. Because Barnevelders are not generally well represented on the show bench, this is a good breed for the novice exhibitor to choose, as there is a fair chance of winning some classes during the first season of showing.

BRABANTER

A crested and muffled breed with a V-shaped horn comb, the Brabanter is thought to be Dutch in origin. It is considered more of an ornamental breed than a practical one, and although the hens lay decent-sized white eggs, these tend to be produced in the spring and early summer only.

Being an ornamental bird, the Brabanter is appealing for its shape, size and colour rather than its egg-laying or meat-producing characteristics. It is found in black, white, spangled, buff, mahogany, cuckoo and lavender colours, and its crest grows vertically, unlike on most other crested breeds, in which the feathers grow horizontally towards the back of the head. In addition, both the male and female have an impressive full throat-beard set between the earmuffs. Of the ornamental breeds, the Brabanter is probably one of the easiest to care for.

BRAHMA

While the most commonly seen Brahma in many countries is the multiple-pencilled partridge or triple-laced variety, other colours include light, dark, Columbian, buff Columbian, cuckoo, birchen, white and gold. Gold cock birds have glossy black breasts, legs and tails, while the hens have delicate black markings on a gold ground colour.

The Brahma originated in India and reached the UK in the mid-1850s, but was recorded in the US roughly a decade earlier. When the birds were first introduced to the UK, they were known as Brahma Poutras and were a great favourite of Prince Albert.

Sometimes known as the 'king of chickens' because of their great size – the cocks can weigh 5kg (11lb) – Brahmas are profusely feathered, staid and matronly in appearance. The feet and legs are heavily feathered and the comb is triple or pea. For a heavy breed, the hens lay a surprising number of light brown eggs each year but, as is often the case with large varieties, these are relatively small in size. Unlike many types of poultry, where one cock bird can easily fertilize six or more hens, Brahmas are best kept as trios if you intend breeding them.

COCHIN

The earliest examples of this breed began to arrive in the UK from the Far East in around 1840. At first the breed assumed different names, presumably because the birds were exported from different places, and it is still sometimes erroneously referred to as the Pekin. In the UK, there is a true bantam known as the Pekin and also a bantam version of the Cochin. In other parts of Europe and in the US, however, only the large Cochin and Cochin bantam are known.

These are big birds and could easily compete with the Brahma for the title of 'king of chickens' as they are comparable in size and weight. The hocks are completely covered in feathers that, unusually, curl around the joints, and the legs and feet are also feathered. The comb is small, single and straight, and in particularly good specimens is well serrated. The eggs are light brown in colour and, for a heavy breed, are quite numerous. The Cochin is classified as being soft-feathered. There are several plumage varieties, the most common being black, white and lavender.

As with all feather-legged breeds, Cochins require special attention, and show birds should always be kept on clean, dry flooring. Nevertheless, they do make a good choice for the novice, especially anyone looking for a breed that will reliably go broody.

CRÈVE-COEUR

The Crève-coeur is one of France's oldest breeds and, like the Bresse, which is the best known of all French chickens, was originally bred as a table bird. Unsurprisingly therefore, the Crève-coeur is classified as a heavy breed. The modern-day bird is larger than its ancestors, owing to the fact that it was crossed with the Dorking from the UK sometime during the 1800s.

The Crève-coeur's head is topped by a full crest, in front of which can be seen a horn comb; like that of the La Flèche (another ancient French breed), this forms a pronounced V shape. Although it is essentially a table bird, the Crève-coeur lays a substantial number of white eggs. As it can also become hand-tame reasonably quickly, it is a good choice for those who want a breed that is a little out of the ordinary. However, its crest can attract lice, so it is important to check it regularly and treat any infestation at the first signs.

CROAD LANGSHAN

Originating from China, this breed was imported to the UK by a Major Croad, after whom it is named. It is sometimes also called the Black Croad Langshan, as although a white strain does exist it is rarely seen, and the black colouring predominates. In Germany, breeders crossed Major Croad's birds with Minorcas and Plymouth Rocks in an effort to achieve a more commercial egg layer, and in doing so developed the separate Langshan breed.

The breed standards classify both Croad Langshans and Langshans as being heavy and soft-feathered. Both have a single comb that should have five points, but while the Langshan has clean legs, the Croad Langshan has sparsely feathered ones. The hens lay well and their eggs are light brown to cream in colour.

DERBYSHIRE REDCAP

Also known simply as the Redcap, this breed is more usually referred to as the Derbyshire Redcap because of its close association with the English county where it originated. The breed was originally produced as a dual-purpose bird, but enthusiasts today prize it for its rarity and for its ability to lay numerous white eggs.

The feathers of the neck, hackle and saddle of the male each have a red quill with beetle-green webbing, finely fringed and tipped with black. The back of the bird is red, while the breast and underparts are black. The hen is more nut-brown in colour, with a black half-moon spangle at the end of each feather. The tail is black in both sexes. The comb is an accentuated rose in shape and has a long, straight leader.

DORKING

Possibly the oldest of English breeds, the Dorking was certainly around at the time of the Roman invasion of Britain in AD 43. Many other breeds were crossed with the Dorking during the 19th century – including the Crève-coeur – to improve their suitability for the table.

Interestingly, the colour variations of silver-grey, red, white and cuckoo dictate the comb type of the Dorking: examples of the silver-grey and red should bear a single comb, while the white and cuckoo must possess a rose comb. Other peculiarities of the breed are its five toes and the pronounced boat shape of its body. The hens lay cream-coloured eggs but generally only in season (spring and summer), so cannot be relied upon for a year-round supply.

The Dorking is classified as soft-feathered and heavy. Some strains of the breed are known to suffer from poor feathering and benefit from being rained on, which will keep the feathers in 'tight' condition. If you are intending to show your birds, however, this will not be possible, as the sun and rain will cause any light or white feathers to turn brassy.

FAVEROLLES

The Faverolles originates in northern France and was bred to be dual-purpose – that is, for both eggs and the table. Nowadays, three distinct types are found: the original French, the German and the British. The breed reached the UK in 1886, since when developments in breed standards have meant that the British type carries its tail higher than its German and French cousins.

Despite their heavy appearance Faverolles are good layers, producing creamy eggs that can sometimes tend towards light brown. The breed has five toes like the Dorking (with which it was crossed to produce a larger bird), lightly feathered legs, a beard and side muffs. The original colour was known as salmon, and in some countries this is still the only colour permitted on the show bench. In Germany and the UK, however, white, black, ermine, blue and Columbian are accepted, while in France the cuckoo colouring is quite common.

FRIESIAN

Classified as a rare breed in the UK by the Rare Poultry Society, the Friesian is a hardy, light, egg-laying breed that originated in the northern parts of the Netherlands. Even the large variety is very small, to the extent that it is not unknown for birds to be entered in bantam classes by mistake.

Friesians produce white eggs, are upright and bold looking, and have quite pronounced white lobes. Their legs are slate blue and the comb is single. Colours can include black, white, red and cuckoo, with the five further varieties – gold, silver, red, lemon and chamois – all being described as pencilled (having numerous small black dots on the feathers of the breast, back and wing shoulders). Although the shape of pencilling varies from breed to breed, in the case of the Friesian the black spots are tiny and teardrop-shaped. As Friesians are light, they are good flyers and it may therefore prove necessary to keep them in an enclosed run to prevent them from roosting in the trees of a neighbour's garden.

FRIZZLE

The Frizzle is Asiatic in origin and is generally thought of as an exhibition breed, the bantam variety having always been more popular than its larger relation. This heavy, soft-feathered bird gets its name from its strange feathering, which should curl towards the head and be as tight and even as possible. In some countries, the word 'frizzle' simply denotes a feather type, but in the UK it is a recognized breed. There is a danger in breeding from the same strain year after year that you will end up with birds that have sparse and weak feathering. To avoid this, do not breed from smooth-feathered cock birds, but instead use a fresh, well-frizzled male to mate with your pullets.

Frizzles come in a range of colours, the most common being black, white, buff, blue and silver-grey. Other permitted but less common colours include Columbian, duckwing, black-red, brown-red, cuckoo, pile and spangle.

Even though it is an exhibition breed, the Frizzle lays reasonably well (the eggs are cream or tinted in colour). Anyone considering keeping these birds should, however, be aware that their feather formation leaves them unable to cope with particularly wet weather, and so they may be better housed indoors.

HAMBURG

Although Hamburgs originated in northern Europe, both spangled and black varieties have been bred for more than 300 years in northern England, where until the mid-19th century they were known as 'Pheasants' and 'Mooneys'. In the UK, Hamburgs are also known as Hollands, whereas in the US Holland is a separate breed. Classified as light, soft-feathered birds, Hamburgs are smart and elegant, with a rose comb and white ear lobes. They lay a reasonable number of white eggs, but are known to be aggressive towards each other if not given sufficient space in the house and run.

Silver Spangled Hamburgs are white with a large black spot at the end of each feather, while Gold Spangled Hamburgs are a rich mahogany colour, with the same black spots. These attractive birds will enhance any garden, although the spangled varieties may become discoloured or brassy if exposed to too much sun. These feathers will eventually moult out, but any suspicion of brassiness would put paid to a bird's show prospects. Pencilled Gold and Silver Hamburgs are created from separate cock-breeder and pullet-breeder strains through a process known as double mating (see page 29).

HOUDAN

Introduced to the UK in the mid-1850s from France, where they were first bred as a table bird, Houdans are now used mainly for exhibition purposes, although they are also reasonably good layers of white eggs. Some poultry standards classify the Houdan as a heavy breed, but this is a mistake and it is in fact light. Its colours are limited, and although white and lavender are seen in some countries, the black mottled variety is most often encountered on the show bench.

The Houdan is heavily crested, probably due to the fact that, generations ago, Crève-coeur blood was introduced to the breed. The distinctive crest, the complete muffling surrounding the face and the leaf-shaped comb (also called a butterfly) together make the Houdan a rarity in the poultry world. To describe the comb further, it is perhaps easier to say that it is in the shape of an oak leaf and looks like two single combs connected only at the point above the beak. As with other crested breeds, the Houdan needs a little extra care in terms of its housing and is best kept indoors or in a covered run. Like the Dorking and Faverolles, it is unusual in having five toes.

INDIAN GAME

Originally bred in Cornwall for cock-fighting, Indian Game birds were subsequently developed for the table through the introduction of blood from foreign breeds brought into the UK by sailors travelling back from Asia. Because of their origins, they are also known as Cornish Game birds, especially in the US. They are classified as heavy and hard-feathered, and possess pea combs and red ear lobes. Only three colours are recognized in the UK: dark (chestnut double-laced with greenish black), jubilee (chestnut laced with white) and blue. Elsewhere, a white laced with chestnut is acceptable.

Indian Game birds are chunky in appearance and, with their widespread legs, look a little like a bulldog when viewed from the front. From above and behind, they are wedge-shaped, with the body tapering down to a short but thickset tail. It is sometimes difficult to breed them with a regular degree of success, as the cock bird often cannot physically manage the mating process owing to his top-heavy build. The male is unusual in being almost monogamous, and so any breeding pens should contain only pairs or trios.

Despite being bred originally as fighters, nowadays Indian Game birds are good-tempered and can become tame, although they will lay only a few eggs in the late spring/early summer months. The eggs they do lay are cream or light brown in colour.

JERSEY GIANT

Another bird that was bred exclusively for the table is the Jersey Giant, which has its origins in North America, where the crossing of Brahmas and Croad Langshans was instrumental in its development. When the bird was first exported to Europe in the 1920s, only the black variety was seen, but today it is also possible to find white and blue-laced birds.

Bigger Jersey Giants are usually produced when stock is bred earlier in the season than is normal, in order that the chicks have the best of the summer months in which to grow. In days gone by, it was not unknown for the breed to live up to its name by producing caponized cock birds weighing as much as 9kg (20lb), although modern strains are nowhere near as heavy. At some stage in the development of the breed, Australorps were also introduced into the bloodline, the result being that, size apart, the two look remarkably similar. Like most heavy breeds, the Jersey Giant makes a fine pet bird and it is also a good layer of brown eggs. However, owing to its size it will need a fair amount of space in which to live.

KO-SHAMO

The Ko-Shamo (also referred to simply as the Shamo) is another hard-feathered breed and has been known for centuries in Japan. It was, until fairly recently, classified in the UK as rare by the Poultry Club. The fact that it is no longer on that list does not mean that its numbers are growing, merely that, along with several other rare hard-feathered breeds, it is now protected by the umbrella of a specialist club.

The breed is unusual in the UK in that even exhibition types have no colour standards. In Europe, however, a number of recognized colours have been standardized, including black, white, red porcelain, blue laced, wheaten, and red- and silver-necked blacks. Three different comb types are allowed, all variations on a theme of small, compact fleshy lumps. Ko-Shamo do not have wattles, but have dewlapped throats instead. The skin on the head and throat is smooth on young birds, but becomes thick and wrinkled after about two years of age.

The birds are easy to manage and, because the cocks are not known for crowing (and, when they do, they don't make much noise), it is possible to have a breeding pen of Ko-Shamos even where neighbours live in close proximity. They are not, unfortunately, gentle with one another, and if two cockerels were to get together there is a good chance that they would fight to the death. Like Indian Game males, Ko-Shamo cock birds are virtually monogamous and should be bred in pairs or trios, kept separate in secure, partitioned runs.

LA FLÈCHE

This old breed takes its name from the town of La Flèche in France. The most peculiar aspect of these birds is their strange comb, which is best described as two small, round horns growing upright and parallel to one another, and which has given rise to the breed's alternative names of 'Devil's Head' and 'Satan's Fowl'.

The breed's original colour was black, but white, cuckoo and blue-laced varieties are now also accepted by the breed standards of most countries. As it was first bred as a table bird, La Flèche is a heavy breed. Despite this, the birds are able to fly well and, if given the chance, will often prefer to roost in any nearby trees rather than an allocated house – substantial covered runs may therefore be necessary.

La Flèches are good layers of large white eggs, but in France they are still kept primarily as meat producers.

LAKENVELDER

Originating in the Dutch/German border region (where its name is spelt Lakenfelder), this is a light breed with a single comb. The plumage patterning is a strong combination of black and white; in some books this is described as 'piebald' or 'belted' owing to the bird's white body and black head and tail, which in good specimens are solid black. The wing feathers should also have some black markings. The Lakenvelder is not easy to breed to show standards, as there is a tendency for white feathers to appear in the neck – something that would be penalized by a judge.

Lakenvelders prefer to live free range and can become quite nervy if they are penned in confined spaces. They are good layers of white eggs and only rarely tend towards broodiness.

LEGHORN

Leghorns have their origins in Italy (Leghorn is the German name for the Italian city of Livorno), but the development of the breed's various forms took place in a number of countries. Large exhibition types are bigger than those bred purely for utilitarian purposes, but even within the exhibition category there are extremes. All possess a large single comb, but to conform to standards the comb of the hen should flop over in British strains, while that of American and Dutch-German types should be slightly smaller and only partially floppy. Rose comb types (as seen in this photograph) are also allowed, despite the fact that they are rare. British Leghorns also have small tails when compared with the Dutch-German large, full-feathered tail and the American spread tail.

The White Leghorn was imported to the UK via the US in the 1870s and the Brown Leghorn followed a few years later. Since then, many other colour variations have been developed. In the UK, black, white, brown, buff, blue and exchequer (a random mix of black and white) are acceptable; in the US, black, white, red, Columbian, partridge, brown, silver partridge and black-tailed red are now regularly seen; while in continental Europe, laced blue, red, yellow, bloodwing silver and cuckoo partridge types are included in the lists of standardized colours. Classified as light and soft-feathered, Leghorns lay a plentiful supply of white eggs.

MALAY

Another Asian hard-feathered breed, the Malay is also quite rare. Good specimens are tall with a long neck and legs, which are accentuated by the sparse plumage. The comb is compact and walnut-shaped, and the wattles are very small. The breed is described in some standards as having a 'cruel and morose expression', which is an appropriate definition.

This large fowl was first seen in the UK in the early 1800s, and for some reason it became particularly popular among breeders in Devon and Cornwall (possibly because of the need to introduce new blood into the Indian Game). The size, shape and character of the Malay is more important than its colour. The shape of the bird is often referred to as 'triple-arched', whereby the first arch is made up of the neck, the second comprises the high-profile wings and the third is formed by the tail, which is carried folded below the horizontal. The white and spangled colour varieties seem to be the most popular in the UK, but black, pile, red porcelain and duckwing are also found in other countries. The birds produce cream-coloured eggs but are not particularly good layers.

MARAN

One of the most remarkable qualities of Marans is the dark, chocolatey colour of their eggs and the fact that, although they are a heavy breed, they lay extremely well. Layers of dark eggs are, however, quite often bred commercially and so will suffer from the wrong leg colour, badly shaped combs and poor feather markings that exclude them from competitive showing and breeding. They are soft-feathered birds and originated in France, where nowadays the breed often has some feathering on its legs.

Often known as Cuckoo Marans because of their colour, birds of this breed are actually found in several varieties, including brassy black, black, white, golden, silver cuckoo and Columbian. In addition, French fanciers also breed a wheaten-coloured bird. The comb is single and medium-sized. Marans are friendly towards people and also to members of their own species, so are suitable both as family pets and for breeding purposes.

MINORCA

The Minorca is similar in appearance to the Leghorn and, like that breed, is a soft-feathered, light bird from the Mediterranean (although the bantam version is a result of breeding in the UK and Germany). Colours are generally limited to black or white, but blues are standardized in most countries and are sometimes seen on the show bench.

The cock usually carries a large, erect, single comb, while that of the hen bird should fold over. In some countries a rose comb is accepted, although in the UK the rose comb bantam version of the Minorca is not permitted as an exhibition breed. All birds should have large, white, oval-shaped ear lobes, but these sometimes suffer from spots and scabs. As the birds reach old age, the white colouring often spreads to the eyelids and face, making it impossible for them to be used for exhibition. The hens are exceptionally good layers of large white eggs and, as the Minorca is also a pretty breed that needs little special attention, it has much to recommend it.

MODERN (ENGLISH) GAME FOWL

This hard-feathered breed was developed in England sometime between 1850 and 1900 as an exhibition bird. It was derived from a cross between the Old English Game and Malay by a generation of judges and breeders who were too young to have had any contact with gamecocks (cock-fighting was abolished in the UK in 1849), and who imagined – totally erroneously – that a bird with more reach would have had the advantage in a fight. With the increasing popularity of showing, judges started looking for taller birds with a shorter hackle and smaller tails. The breed that was developed was originally known as the Exhibition Modern Game but the word 'exhibition' was later dropped.

The comb of the Modern Game is single and small, and the breed is found in several colour varieties, including birchen, golden birchen, partridge, white bloodwing, silver bloodwing, black, blue and white. Its most notable features are its long legs, elongated neck and overall carriage, which are all important if you intend to try your luck on the show bench. Modern Game birds are not brilliant layers, but because they are small and elegant and soon become very tame, they make excellent pets for the suburban poultry keeper.

NEW HAMPSHIRE RED

Always a favourite in its native US, but also rapidly gaining popularity in the UK, the New Hampshire Red is thought to have been bred from the Rhode Island Red without the introduction of any other blood. The birds are, however, lighter in colour than Rhode Island Reds, and are classed as heavy and soft-feathered. The breed is probably best accepted as being dual-purpose, although it was originally bred as a layer.

New Hampshire Reds are popular competition birds, especially in northern Europe, and are an excellent breed for the novice as a single colour (in this case chestnut-red) is easier to breed to exhibition level. They also have a placid nature and make perfect family pets, and as they are good layers they will keep a family in brown eggs for a good proportion of the year.

OLD ENGLISH GAME

Like the Modern Game, the light, hard-feathered Old English has its origins in Britain and was tremendously popular as a fighting bird. Over the years some 30 colours have been known in this large breed, and in several countries any non-defined colour variations can be shown, as the judges are more interested in body shape and muscle tone. The overall appearance should be of a well-rounded, muscular bird, which is heart-shaped when viewed from above. Occasionally, rumpless varieties of the breed are also seen. Traditionally, the small, single comb of the male birds was 'dubbed', or trimmed, to prevent injuries when fighting, but this practice is now illegal in many countries.

Although Old English Game birds are aggressive towards each other, their boldness is a positive attribute when they are kept as pets, because they soon become tame. To help them stay fit and active, they are best kept free range. Old English are probably the best layers of all the hard-feather breeds and produce a cream-coloured egg.

ORLOFF

The Orloff is unusual in that it is one of the few poultry breeds to have originated in Russia, although the bantamized form was created in Germany in the early part of the 20th century. In fact, the large breed is now probably less popular amongst fanciers than the dwarf or miniature version.

American show standards recognize three colour varieties, but in the UK four are accepted, the best known of which is the mahogany (classified elsewhere as red porcelain). The Orloff has a walnut comb and a short, thick beak, and it stands tall on yellow legs. Both sexes have a full beard and bushy eyebrows. The birds are soft-feathered and come under the classification of a heavy breed – the large fowl was originally dual-purpose.

Perhaps as a result of their Russian origins, Orloffs are known to be hardy and are unfazed by inclement weather conditions. The hens lay a good number of cream-coloured eggs and, when broody, make reliable and caring mothers.

ORPINGTON

The Orpington makes a good beginner's bird and is popular throughout the world. When the black variety was first introduced at the London Dairy Show in October 1886, it produced quite a stir. Within five years, however, it had been joined by white and buff varieties, and other breeders were crossing Croad Langshan and Cochin breeds and passing them off as Black Orpingtons, such was the demand. Today, the four self-colours (buff, blue, black and white) are equally attractive and are almost the only variations ever seen
in the UK. Elsewhere, birchen, buff-black laced, barred (or cuckoo), Columbian and partridge types are also quite common.

The Orpington is a soft-feathered, heavy bird and is known to lay a good number of light brown eggs. It has a small single comb, although the black variety sometimes has a rose comb. Its friendly, docile nature should make either the large fowl or the bantam a strong contender as the choice of breed for the first-time chicken keeper.

POLAND

The Poland has a huge ball-like feather crest and a small, sometimes completely absent, horned comb in front. Interestingly, its name is derived from the English word 'polled', rather than from the country of Poland. As defined in the US, the UK, Germany, the Netherlands and several other countries, the breed is divided into two groups: the White Crested, with normal wattles; and the Paduaner, which is bearded. Nowadays, the colouring of the first group is restricted to black, blue or cuckoo barred, while the latter group includes gold and silver laced, chamois, black, blue and white.

To maintain the crests of Polands in good order, the birds should be kept under cover when it is raining and special drinkers should be used. If you have small pens of birds, nipple drinkers or aviary-type drinkers are best, but with larger flocks it is not a bad idea to use old-fashioned pottery pigeon drinkers or even dog bowls covered with a screen of wire netting. While Polands do need special care, novices should not be put off by the potential extra work involved. The birds are classified as light and soft-feathered, and they lay white eggs.

PLYMOUTH ROCK

This is an American breed, but the modern-day British type is taller and different in shape from birds found in the US. In the UK, the barred (thought to have been a result of breeding with the Scots Grey) and buff varieties are perhaps the most commonly seen nowadays, but other colours such as partridge, Columbian, buff Columbian and blue laced are also accepted. In the US the original Plymouth Rock has become known as the Barred Rock, and the breed has subsequently been further divided by colour. As a point of interest, the barring in the US variety is broader than that seen on examples in the UK. Similarly, in the US the black bars in the hens are broader than the white, while bars of equal width are desired in the cocks. The black should be beetle green/black in colour and it should not be possible to confuse the birds with the Black Rock, which was developed as a commercial breed and is often found with a tinge of brown in its plumage.

The Plymouth Rock is a heavy breed with soft feathers, and any of the variations would make a good choice for the novice. They are good layers of cream-coloured eggs (described as 'yellowish' in the US).

RHODE ISLAND RED

Known simply as the Rhode Island in its native US, this breed is generally given the suffix 'red' in the UK and in other countries where a white variety is also found. In the red strains, the comb can be either single (most commonly seen) or a rose, but in the white a rose comb is considered more correct. Confusingly, in the US whites and reds are regarded as two different breeds. The red variety is much darker in colour than the New Hampshire Red but is otherwise very similar in stance and formation.

Like New Hampshire Reds, Rhode Island Reds are hardy and are happy to adapt to almost any healthy surroundings. These highly recommended birds are also excellent layers of light brown eggs.

SCOTS DUMPY

This breed, whose name is sometimes spelt Scots Dumpie, is very old and may even have been brought to Scotland before the Roman invasion of Britain in AD 43. In its cuckoo colouring, the hen could perhaps be mistaken for a Maran, although the cock bird is much finer and has a different shape altogether. Because of their noticeably short legs, the birds have a distinctive waddling gait quite unlike that of other chickens. The reason for their short legs and heavy body is traditionally attributed to the fact that Scottish crofts and smallholdings were surrounded by wild countryside in which predators were rife, so the birds were bred this way to encourage them to stay close to home.

At one time the Dumpy came in a range of colours, but unfortunately, owing to a loss of genetic material, only black, white and cuckoo varieties are seen today. Had it not been for a dedicated band of breeders in the 1970s, the Scots Dumpy could have died out altogether. The birds are classified as a light breed and have a single comb, and the tail of the cock is full and flowing. The hen is considered to be an excellent broody and mother, and lays cream-coloured eggs.

SCOTS GREY

The Scots Grey was popular in Scotland until around the 1930s, when the breed seemed to lose favour among chicken keepers in its own country. The breed standard recognizes only the cuckoo variety, and insists that it should have a 'single comb' and 'white mottled legs', and be a 'fine, compact, smart bird with well-defined markings'. It resembles the Scots Dumpy in appearance, and its single comb is similarly accompanied by red ear lobes. Both breeds would make a good choice for the beginner. The Scots Grey lays tinted eggs.

SILKIE

Silkies are a light breed that arrived in the UK from China sometime in the early 1800s. Since then, they have become extremely popular and are often given to children as pets – there is no doubt that their unusual feathering fascinates youngsters. Colours include white, black, partridge, cuckoo, red buff and lavender, although not all of these are recognized everywhere.

The comb is known as a mulberry or cushion, and is almost circular in shape but preferably broader rather than long. The male has a slightly spiky crest while that of the female should be short and neat, resembling a powder puff. Some strains also have a beard. Both the male and female have an extra toe at the back of each foot. Also typical of the breed is the blue-black skin colour.

Silkies are docile and easy to keep, but because of their feathering they should always have access to a dry run and warm housing. They lay a creamy brown egg and can be expected to produce an average of 105 eggs before going broody. The breed is particularly useful for crossing with others to produce the ideal surrogate mother.

SUMATRA

Members of this breed have long tails, making them unsuited to wet, muddy conditions and necessitating large houses with high perches. Having said that, they are slender, graceful, striking birds that possess a dark blue triple or pea comb – this colouring is referred to by some breeders as 'gypsy'. Red combs, faces and wattles are sometimes seen, but they are not desirable on the show bench. Another unusual feature of the breed is that the cock bird will often grow more than one spur on each leg. Generally, only two colours are seen – blue and black – but in Germany a white strain was developed by mating a Sumatra with a Yokohama. Elsewhere, there is also a black-red variety.

If you are tempted to keep Sumatras, bear in mind you should confine them in large grassy runs or, better still, give them total free range, although be aware that they may prefer to roost in any surrounding trees rather than in their allocated home. Unusually for poultry that originates in Asia, the Sumatra lays white eggs.

SUSSEX

The well-known Sussex, which originated from the Speckled Barn at around the time of the Roman invasion of England in AD 43, was originally a table bird but is now dual purpose. Outbreeding with Cochin blood probably produced the first Light Sussex and as a result the colour of the eggs became tinted and the numbers produced greatly improved. Some fanciers do not regard the Light Sussex as a true variety, and in a number of countries it is known by its colour, Columbian. The breed also consists of six other types: speckled, buff, white, silver, brown and red. A cuckoo variety is also allowed in some parts of the world.

The plumage variations of the Sussex can be difficult to achieve to show standard, but that should not put anyone off trying one of the less common colours. Note also that if the lighter shades are being shown they need to be kept out of sunlight to prevent them from turning brassy. The breed has a single comb and a good, solid body, making it full of character and giving it the look of a typical 'farmyard' bird. The hens are also excellent layers despite being classified as a heavy breed.

TWENTE

Twente, or Twense, is the Dutch name for a breed that is also known by its German name of Kraienköppe and was developed on the borders of the two countries. Although not particularly well known in the UK, where it is classified as a rare breed, the Twente is popular in its countries of origin. The birds are good looking, with a proud, erect stance, not unlike that of the Old English Game. The comb is walnut shaped in the male but hardly exists at all in the female. Colours are partridge, silver partridge, blue partridge and silver-blue partridge, although in the UK the two varieties known are called gold and silver.

The birds are robust and hardy, and soon become tame towards humans, but unfortunately are sometimes aggressive towards each other. The hens are good layers. Both large fowl and bantam types lay cream-coloured eggs and the large fowl type are known for laying right through winter, unlike some other breeds.

WELSUMMER

This Dutch breed takes its name from the village of Welsum and has blood from the Cochin, Wyandotte, Leghorn, Barnevelder and Rhode Island Red breeds in its make-up. In most countries the Welsummer is found in only one colour, which in the male is similar to that of a black-red Old English Game and in the hen to that of a Brown Leghorn. Unlike other black-red birds such as the Brown Leghorn and Partridge Wyandotte, which have pure black breasts, the Welsummer has a breast that is a mixture of brown and black, similar to that of a pullet-breeder Partridge Wyandotte.

The birds have a single comb and are classified as a soft-feathered, light breed. Compared to other egg-laying breeds, Welsummers are relatively poor layers, but the dark brown colour of their eggs is comparable to that of the Maran, the only difference being that the shell of the Maran is glossy whereas that of a Welsummer is matt.

Interestingly, the darkest eggs often come from poor layers, while the better layers produce lighter coloured eggs. Therefore if the breeder selects hatching eggs that are deep chocolate in colour, he may unwittingly also be selecting for low egg production in the future.

WYANDOTTE

The soft-feathered, heavy Wyandotte breed originated in the US as the Silver Laced Wyandotte. The feather lacing came about by crossing a Silver Sebright bantam with either a Cochin or a Brahma and then introducing a Silver Spangled Hamburg. The white variety is a sport of the Silver Laced Wynadotte and was developed in the UK before being exported back to the US, where it was further improved to become an excellent layer of white or cream-coloured eggs.

The breed has at least 14 colour variations in the UK alone, and at least 22 in total around the world. It is not, however, just the variety of colours or the general appearance of the birds that makes them so popular, but rather their ease of keeping. Some of the colour variations do make for complicated breeding problems – the partridge variety, for example, is produced through the process of double mating (see page 29), for which separate pens of pullet- and cock-breeding birds are required. Like many other pale-coloured breeds, the White Wyandotte needs protection from the sun if you intend to exhibit birds, but even so it is perhaps the best variety for the beginner.

YOKOHAMA

The long-tailed Yokohama cannot be mistaken for any other breed. In a mature bird the tail can easily reach 60cm (2ft) in length, and in Japan (where the breed originated) fanciers keep the birds in conditions that prevent them from moulting to encourage the tail to grow as much as 1m (3ft) each year. Both single and walnut combs are accepted in the breed standards. The former is most often seen in black-red and duckwing colorations, while the latter is more common in red-saddled and white varieties.

Keeping Yokohama cock birds in prime condition can be a little difficult, and to maintain perfect show specimens you do need taller houses and higher perches than would normally be necessary. The laying capabilities of this light, ornamental breed can be quite varied. Depending on the strain, some hens will lay only 40–50 eggs in a season, while others can average somewhere around 100.

Where & When
to Get Your Chickens

Once you have decided on the breed and type of chicken you prefer, you need to find a supplier of good-quality birds. Poultry shows and poultry magazines are good sources of information when it comes to finding contact details for reliable breeders, but where possible it is best to obtain your stock through word-of-mouth recommendations. Even so, breeders are unlikely to sell you their very best birds, as they will want to keep these to maintain their own strains.

Buying and Sourcing Birds

In addition to publications aimed specifically at the poultry keeper, the classified section of your local newspaper may contain advertisements for poultry. Birds are quite often sold as trios (one cock and two hens), but in some countries a numerical code may be used to describe what exactly is on offer. Such an advertisement may include the name of the breed, followed by '1–2', denoting one cock and two hens; '1–0', telling you that a single cockerel is on offer; or '0–3', indicating that three hens or pullets are looking for a new home. Do not be confused by numbers like '06' at the end of the advert, as these merely indicate the year in which the chickens were bred rather than the quantity on sale.

If you have set your heart on a particular breed you may have to travel some distance to find it, but with effort and perseverance you will eventually source exactly what you want.

RIGHT Some poultry shows include 'selling' classes, which can be a good way of obtaining new stock.

Useful Organizations

From your initial enquiries about local poultry breeders, you should also be able to find out the whereabouts of your local poultry club. In some cases these are general fanciers' societies, combining all manner of fur and feather (rabbits, guinea pigs, pigeons and so on) rather than chickens and bantams specifically, although usually the majority of their members are, in fact, poultry keepers and breeders.

The addresses of clubs and societies devoted to specific breeds can be found in specialist poultry-keeping magazines or through the national poultry clubs. In the UK, these are the Poultry Club of Great Britain and the Rare Poultry Society (see box), while in the US, the American Bantam Association and American Poultry Association are on hand to answer questions. The breed clubs generally hold shows and exhibitions several times a year, and these are always good venues at which to make specific enquiries about purchasing birds and to gain general advice. Sometimes they also include selling classes, which are perhaps the best way to obtain your desired stock.

Most of the clubs have websites, and in addition to these there are many other poultry-oriented websites that offer chickens for sale, information on breeds, and noticeboard links where you can post your requests or simply communicate with other like-minded enthusiasts.

Useful Addresses

Poultry Club of Great Britain
South Lodge
Creeton Road
Swinstead
Grantham
Lincolnshire
NG33 4PG
tel: 01476 550067
www.poultryclub.org

Rare Breeds Survival Trust
National Agricultural Centre
Stoneleigh Park
Warwickshire
CV8 2LZ
tel: 024 7669 6551
www.rbst.org.uk

Rare Poultry Society
Danby
The Causeway
Congresbury
Bristol
BS49 5DJ
tel: 01934 833619

Utility Poultry Breeders Association
Morville Heath
Bridgenorth
Shropshire
tel: 01661 844961
www.utilitypoultry.co.uk

The Age to Buy Your Birds

If your chosen breed proves difficult to find, or if your finances will not permit the purchase of adult pure-bred birds, you might consider purchasing a small pen of bantams to use as surrogate mothers to hatch fertile eggs instead. Such birds should be easy to source almost anywhere in your locality, but they must be the right sort: heavy in appearance, placid and reasonable egg layers. As they go broody (which they certainly will), you can set fertile eggs bought from a known breeder beneath them to hatch. Fertile eggs for hatching in this way can be bought and transported over long distances much more cheaply than mature stock. It might sound highly risky to entrust such a fragile parcel to a postal or private delivery service but, provided the eggs are carefully packed, there are rarely any breakages.

Another option is to buy day-old chicks and rear them using bantams in the same way. Many of the larger poultry breeders hatch their eggs by artificial incubation and are quite happy to sell chicks to chicken fanciers, who can then bring them to maturity either by rearing them under broody hens or with the aid of electric or gas brooders. Where possible, the chicks should be collected in person but, like eggs, day-olds do not seem to suffer unduly by being transported by rail or road. For the hours spent in transit, the chicks can generate enough body heat to keep themselves sufficiently warm, helped by the fact that they are carried in specially designed, insulated boxes. The methods of introducing eggs or day-old chicks to a broody hen are described in Breeding Chickens, page 102.

Purchasing adult birds obviously has its advantages. Not least, there is unlikely to be the frustration of rearing young chicks to maturity, only to find that they are either nearly all cockerels and therefore unable to supply eggs, or, if showing is your ultimate goal, sub-quality specimens that do not quite conform to the breed standards. Birds bought at point-of-lay or beyond can be placed in the chicken shed and run immediately, and do not require any intermediate housing or extra care. And the maintenance costs of adult birds are lower as there is no need to provide heating, chick crumbs or growers' pellets.

A pullet is a female bird that is in its first year and has yet to commence laying, while a hen is generally accepted as being an older female that has completed her first season of laying. From the point of view of buying birds, pullets are a better choice than hens as you will obviously gain more eggs from them over the course of their lifetime. Having said that, if eggs are your main objective there is no reason why you should not consider buying hens that have been discarded by commercial set-ups after their first season, as these birds are usually inexpensive and still have plenty of laying potential ahead of them.

When contacting breeders initially, it is important to state whether you want pullets or hens. Likewise, when selecting a male bird, specify either a cockerel (under 18 months) or an older cock bird.

When to Buy

In addition to selling surplus birds at shows, poultry clubs often organize poultry sales and auctions. When these are held in the early spring, you can be sure that the majority of birds on offer will be around a year old and in peak condition for breeding or just ready for a long life of egg-laying. Sales held in the autumn may contain young birds bred in the same year or older birds that, while they might be past their prime for showing purposes, are nevertheless still capable of producing eggs or show-quality offspring in the next rearing season.

Generally speaking, at autumn sales it makes sense to buy stock that has been hatched in the spring of the same year. By the time they are sold, such birds can be kept as adults and should lay, if somewhat sporadically (unless they are a commercial breed), throughout the winter months before really getting into their stride the following spring. Show birds of this age will also be at their peak for breeding and exhibition purposes the following year.

If you are not buying at spring and autumn sales, just choose the best birds as and when they are on offer. However, remember that chicks or young birds always do better and grow more vigorously during the summer months, when they have access to fresh grass and more sun on their backs.

LEFT Chicks bought day-old need to be reared under a foster mother or artificial brooder.

ABOVE A clear, bright, well-pigmented eye is a good indicator of healthy stock.

What to Look For

By purchasing stock from reputable breeders or at sales organized by a club or society, you can be reasonably confident that only well-kept and healthy birds are on offer. It is, however, very useful to be able to recognize the typical signs of a healthy bird from its overall appearance.

First, the comb and wattles must be bright and waxy. There are a few exceptions to this rule, such as when the breed has an unusually coloured comb (for example, the Silkie), or when a hen has been brooding chicks or is in moult and not laying. Second, the eyes should be clear and bright and the plumage shiny and full. During the summer, you may notice broken feathers on the back and neck of females in a breeding pen, but this will probably have been caused by the mating cock bird.

Handle any bird you consider buying, as even the breeds classified as light should feel fleshy and well muscled. Check the breastbone – it should be reasonably well covered with flesh and certainly not sharp like a knife blade. Inspect the vent (anal area) for signs of diarrhoea and for lice and mites. The underpart of the wings nearest the body is another area favoured by parasites, so lift up the wings, gently brush back the fine feathers in the opposite direction to their growth and look carefully for movement – although tiny, fleas, lice and mites are all visible to the naked eye.

Finally, spend some time watching the flock: they should all be busy scratching around, dusting in the earth, feeding or preening. Avoid buying birds from a pen where even just one individual is moping around or is isolated from the rest of the batch, as this could be a sign of disease and at the very least indicates that all is not well. Also look around the pen to ensure the faeces are firm, well formed and, in part, white in colour. Slimy, watery green or yellowish diarrhoea-like droppings are another indicator of ill health.

Getting Your Birds Home

Before setting out to collect your carefully chosen chickens, make sure that the henhouse and run are ready for their arrival and that food and water are in place. It pays to ask the breeder in advance what type of feedstuffs your new birds are used to and, if possible, to purchase your food from the same manufacturer. Alternatively, ask the breeder if you can take home some food so that you can make the changeover to a new supply gradually.

If possible, borrow a proper poultry crate or basket for transporting the birds. Otherwise, arm yourself with a sturdy cardboard box that has plenty of air holes and a decent lid to deter escapees. Removing the flaps at the top of the box and replacing them with a piece of hardboard cut fractionally oversize can make for a more secure lid. Construct hinges and fasteners by threading wire or string through small holes drilled in the box and lid. Hay or straw makes a better covering for the base of a box than wood shavings, as it allows the chickens a better grip. If you are intending to buy birds from a public sale, animal welfare officers may be in attendance to check that your box conforms to any government regulations regarding livestock transportation.

Once home, keep the chickens confined to their house for a few hours so that they can become accustomed to their new surroundings. When they appear settled (after a few hours in the day or overnight), lift the pop-hole and let them explore the run area. Don't push them out, as it is better to let them make their own way so that they don't become disoriented. If the house has no confining run, leave the birds shut in for 24 hours before giving them free range.

Make every effort to get acquainted with your chickens straight away. Always move slowly and spend some time crouching at the feeder, so that hunger and interest will ensure they approach you. Before long, they will quite literally be eating out of your hand.

BELOW Transport birds in a strong container that is not be too big for its occupants, otherwise they will slide about in transit.

Housing
& Cleaning

How your chickens are housed depends on considerations such as the space available, the breed you have chosen and the number of birds. While the initial cost of a good housing system is high, it will last a lifetime of chicken keeping, particularly if it is well maintained. One option is to build your own unit, which can be tailor-made to suit your requirements and to fit a particular part of your garden or smallholding. Alternatively, there is a wide range of commercially produced housing units on the market, many at reasonable prices.

ABOVE The best of all worlds: this unit provides shade in the summer and shelter in wet weather, and allows access to the garden when convenient.

Space Requirements

The amount of space required for housing your birds depends to some extent on the method of rearing you adopt. If chickens are given access to a large outdoor space, they will spend very little time in the house, using it only on wet days and for roosting or egg-laying. However, if the birds are kept intensively, the combined floor space of their house and run will need to be greater, as they will spend all their time there and will require sufficient room for feeding, roosting, nesting and exercising. Whatever system you choose, the basic premise is that you should give your flock enough room to ensure that the three H's – health, happiness and hygiene – are all maintained.

If you intend to keep your chickens intensively, a house measuring 1.5 x 2m (5 x 7ft) should be sufficient for six hens; if a run is attached, it will accommodate 12 birds. For these sorts of numbers, a combined house and run area of 5sq m (6sq yd) per bird is adequate, although much will depend on whether you are keeping bantams, light large fowl or any of the extremely heavy breeds such as Croad Langshans or Brahmas.

It is also important to remember that, unless you keep your poultry-keeping operation very small, one house and run is

RIGHT AND BELOW A raised chicken house offers some essential shade, and with a little ingenuity its appearance can enhance rather than detract from the garden.

unlikely to be enough. There will be times when extra space will have to be found to accommodate a broody hen and her chicks, a 'resting' cockerel or a sick bird. If you intend exhibiting your stock, you will also need a separate penning shed where birds can be kept clean and 'trained' to show themselves to their best advantage. In addition, a shed or some kind of food store may be required.

Types of Housing

If you are keeping just a few birds, a movable combined house and run (sometimes known as an ark or fold unit) is probably your best option. You will, however, need sufficient space to be able to keep moving the run on to fresh ground before the area beneath it turns into a mud-bath, something that is particularly important during the wetter months of the year. The alternative to the movable unit is a permanent house and run.

Movable Housing

If you have enough space to move a fold unit on to fresh grass every few days, then this is arguably a better option than a permanent hen-house and probably creates the least amount of work. Some units have exterior-opening nest-boxes and, in a few cases, attached feeders and drinkers that can be accessed from the outside, thereby obviating the need to enter the shelter other than to clean out the floor litter in the roosting compartment periodically. The chickens can be kept confined but still have access to fresh grass, and, if the unit is moved on a regular basis, there is little chance of a build-up of disease. The chickens can still be allowed free range when you are around, but they are protected from predators and dogs when you are not.

The housing part of a fold unit usually takes up about a third of the overall length, with the remainder forming the run. Traditionally, the units are A-framed, with one door allowing access to the house and another to the run. As an added refinement, the back of the run may be fully or partially covered to provide the birds with shade from the sun and shelter from the rain. Old-fashioned fold units, as once used by the commercial poultry industry, are still sometimes seen and are often equipped with wheels that make moving them easier. Most modern-day versions, however, merely have a carrying pole (usually running along the apex of the roof if the unit is triangular) or extending handles at each corner. A strong floor is essential. The base of the unit rests constantly on damp grass and so needs to be thick enough to withstand moisture and being dragged on to fresh ground regularly.

If you have only a trio of birds or half a dozen bantams, an oversized rabbit-hutch type unit is ideal. One-third comprises a wooden-floored roosting and nesting section, while the remaining two-thirds has no floor, giving the occupants access to fresh grass. As only the front of the run section is wired, this type of housing is totally wind- and waterproof and so would be worth considering if you intend to keep light-coloured exhibition birds. Some designs also permit the whole roof to slide back on runners, which makes routine maintenance very easy indeed.

For some of the true bantams or miniaturized breeds, an actual rabbit hutch might make a good home. The birds would, however, need access to a small exercise pen or should periodically be given free range to roam the garden.

ABOVE AND RIGHT A movable fold unit is the perfect answer in a small garden, as it can be moved every few days, giving the hens regular access to fresh grass while allowing the previous patch to recover. Within larger set-ups the unit can be used as a pen for breeding birds or laying hens, or as a rearing unit for a broody and her chicks.

Permanent Housing

The Victorians were very keen on poultry keeping and often made a feature of their hen-houses in the same way that dovecotes evolved to become ornamental. Poultry houses usually took the form of a lean-to along the side of a walled garden or stable yard, and generally consisted of a shed and run, with the roof of the shed continuing over the run section. Separate doors allowed access to either the house or the run, the floor of which was normally constructed of compounded earth. Straw, peat or dried bracken was spread over the floor and grain was sprinkled in this litter to keep the hens busy.

If you have the space and a suitable wall that is not too close to your own house or

LEFT AND RIGHT Pop-holes need to be easily accessible and large enough for your stock to get through, while offering nighttime security from predators.

that of your neighbour, it might be possible to consider a variation on this theme. If you replaced the floor covering with sand, such a set-up would be ideal for some of the heavily leg- and feet-feathered breeds. The covered run also makes it perfect for light- or white-coloured exhibition birds, which become brassy if exposed to the sun or inclement weather.

A large conventional hen-house can often be partitioned to allow several pens of birds to be kept under the same roof. The only disadvantage to this is that a narrow corridor needs to be constructed through the interior of the shed, so that the daily chores can be carried out from the inside, thereby removing the possibility of having two runs – one on either side of the building.

Instead of buying a commercially available hen-house, you could adapt an existing outbuilding. As mentioned above, a shed measuring 1.5 x 2m (5 x 7ft) is adequate for about six large hens, or up to 12 if it opens on to a decent-sized run. It will need to be light, airy, well ventilated and predator-proof, and the door should open and close easily, as you will need to use it several times each day for access. Brush away any cobwebs on the inside of the shed, wash the windows and, if necessary, paint the walls to make it brighter.

It is important that you take the possibility of hot summers into account if you are planning to use an existing structure in which to house your birds. Old stone buildings are well insulated from the sun, but more modern sheds may become stifling in the heat of the day.

Structural Considerations

Whether you are designing your own hen-house or purchasing a ready-made unit, it is important to bear the requirements of your chosen breed in mind. If you intend to keep a long-tailed breed such as the Yokohama, for example, the house needs to be tall enough to contain perches fixed at such a height that the birds' long, flowing tails will not be damaged when they are at roost. Likewise, a house with a pop-hole only 30cm (12in) square might suit bantams, but it will make it impossible for a large Buff Orpington to exit or enter.

Nor should houses be bought for the convenience of the chickens alone. If you have a bad back, for instance, you will not enjoy having to get down on your hands and knees every time you need to feed your chickens, collect their eggs or clean out the roosting compartment of a small ark unit. For the same reason, permanent housing must be at least 1.5m (5ft) high to allow easy access for all those important day-to-day chores. A tall building also has the benefit of improved airflow and ventilation, both very important factors in chicken keeping (see next page).

The floor of a permanent hen-house must be sufficiently strong and adequately braced to prevent springiness as you walk on it; this is especially important when it is raised off the ground. Raised houses must also be equipped with a gangplank leading up to the pop-hole in order to prevent possible injuries to the chickens' legs and feet as they enter and exit.

Windows and Ventilation

Good ventilation in the hen-house is vital in preventing respiratory diseases, and can be provided by natural means such as windows and/or a protected open ridge running along the roof apex. It must be possible to open the windows, but if there is any danger that predators or vermin can get in through them, they should be covered with small-mesh wire netting on the interior of the building. Approximately one-fifth of the available wall space should be given over to windows.

In the summer, warm, stale air inside the hen-house leads to an increased incidence of disease, so ventilation is crucial. In winter, when temperatures are cooler, ventilation of the house is necessary only to get rid of stale air and to prevent the accumulation of ammonia gas (generated from droppings), and usually takes place incidentally through the opening of doors and through cracks under the roof eaves. The main problem at this time of year is preventing draughty conditions, something chickens cannot tolerate.

Nest-Boxes

The hen-house should contain some simple nest-boxes, ideally one for every three laying birds you intend to keep. Each box should measure 30cm (12in) square

and be around 35cm (14in) high. They may be made in tiers, in which case an alighting perch should be attached to the front of each box.

The boxes should be placed just off the ground and in the darkest part of the house (usually under the windows), as chickens prefer a quiet, dim place in which to lay their eggs. Straw or hay makes a good liner to nest-boxes, but it will need to be cleaned out regularly and dusted with louse powder. Remove any broken eggs immediately to discourage egg-eating, a habit that, once formed, is very hard to stop (see page 98).

Types of Bedding

Whatever materials have been used to build the hen-house floor, a covering of litter is essential. It serves three main purposes: to absorb the birds' droppings; to provide ground-level insulation; and to give the birds plenty of exercise and interest. Types of bedding include:

Wood shavings – the most common form of litter, available in compressed bales from suppliers of horse feeds and equipment. If you manage to source your own local supply from a firm making wood-based products, check that the shavings are safe to use (softwoods are best) and that they have not been treated with toxic or irritant chemicals. Because sawdust is fine and is made even more so by the birds' constant scratching, it may cause respiratory problems and so should be avoided.

•

Shredded newspaper – available in bales from most agricultural stockists. This makes perfect bedding material as it is highly absorbent, contains no parasites and can be burnt or added to the compost heap after use. The only disadvantage of newspaper is that it is so lightweight – on a windy day the surrounding area can end up looking as though a ticker-tape parade has just taken place.

•

Straw – probably even easier to obtain than shredded newspaper in rural areas, as most farmers will be able to sell you a bale or two after harvest. Wheat straw is best, as it is most durable, but oat straw is a good second choice. Although chopped straw is more absorbent and is preferred by chickens, it can, like sawdust, become dusty and affect the birds' respiratory system. You should never use hay, as it mats together into a carpet and has also been known to make birds crop-bound (see page 116). It can, however, be used in nest-boxes or when forming a comfortable base for a broody hen to hatch fertile eggs.

•

Leaves – collected in the autumn. Birds will happily scratch around in these. At one time, peat was favoured by poultry keepers, but it is very dusty unless kept damp and its collection is not environmentally friendly.

•

Silver or sharp sand – may prove to be the best floor covering if you keep a feather-legged breed. Ask your intended stock supplier what he or she uses and go with this recommendation.

Whatever litter you choose, make sure that it is not mouldy or damp. Mould can cause serious respiratory diseases, while wet litter is a perfect breeding ground for the *E. coli* bacterium. The litter base should be about 12–15cm (5–6in) deep and needs to be raked over daily to remove any matted portions, such as under the perches and around water drinkers. In addition, a complete renewal of the litter will be necessary every five or six months (see page 78).

Occasionally, new birds try to roost inside nest-boxes, but this must be discouraged or foul nests and dirty eggs will result. When the chickens are first placed in the hen-house, prevent them from roosting in the nest-boxes at night by covering up the fronts of the boxes with a board or a curtain of sacking. It is also a good idea to make the tops of the boxes inaccessible at night by covering each with a steeply sloping board.

If you want to get into serious egg production, consider using trap nests, as they are the surest way of telling how well an individual bird is laying. The trap closes when a hen enters the nest to lay, so she cannot get out until she is let out. Combined with the use of leg rings or wing tags to identify the individual birds, trap nests allow a record to be kept of all the eggs each hen lays. The system demands that the house is visited every two to three hours, but for those who have the time the results can be very interesting.

Perches

One or two perches running the length of the hen-house will give your chickens or bantams somewhere to roost at night. If you need to install more than one perch, be sure to keep them at the same height or the birds will all try to roost on the higher one.

The thickness and width of a perch depends on whether you intend to keep bantams or large fowl, but should not be so narrow as to cause damage to the birds' breastbones. For bantams, the perch should be about 5cm (2in) wide and 3cm (1in) thick, while large birds require something slightly more substantial – their perches should be around 8cm (3in) wide and perhaps 5cm (2in) thick. In all cases, the top edges must be rounded off. Always try to use planed wood for perches and

never use any wood that has bark attached: rough-sawn timber can cause splinters, while a covering of bark provides an ideal home for avian parasites such as red mite (see page 117). Both types of wood are also difficult to scrape clean.

At least 20cm (8in) of perching space should be allocated to each bird, and if a single perch is being used in a large poultry house it should be supported every 1.8m (6ft) of its length. The height at which the perches are fixed is also very important. Unless you are keeping long-tailed breeds (which require a higher roosting point), perches fixed at around 60cm (2ft) off the floor are about as high as you should consider, although for some of the heavier breeds such as Croad Langshans, 30cm (1ft) is perfect. Perches should not be too high – even for the lighter, flightier breeds – because the pads of the birds' feet can be injured by constant hard landings each morning. There is also a danger that sudden jarring may upset the hens' reproductive system. Where a droppings board is used, it can be set at around the heights recommended above for perches and the perch then constructed about 15cm (6in) above it.

If you are housing exhibition birds, it is particularly important that their tails do not become damaged by constant brushing against the interior wall. The distance between the wall and the intended perch position should therefore take this factor into account. Perches must also never be attached permanently to the walls of the house. Instead, they should be fitted into slotted grooves, hooked into brackets or built as a free-standing frame. In this way, they can be removed for regular cleaning and disinfecting, and they can also be taken out altogether if the house is required for a broody hen or for young stock.

Runs and Fencing

The fencing used to form a run around permanent poultry buildings should be around 2m (6ft 6in) high, not only to contain flighty birds but, more importantly, to keep predators out. In practice, the chicken wire most commonly used for this type of fencing has a 19-gauge thickness and 5cm (2in) mesh, and measures 1.8m (6ft) across the roll. The fence posts should be around 4m (12ft) apart. About 30cm (1ft) of the fencing wire must be dug into the ground to prevent pests or predators from scratching their way in or the chickens from pushing their way out, and unless the top of the pen is covered with a nylon net (see below), brackets of about 1m (3ft) should be attached to the top of each fence post on the outside. Three strands of barbed wire (or electric wire, for which you will need a fencing unit) can then be affixed to each bracket quite tightly, and this will prevent most predators from climbing into the pen.

A nylon net can be used to form a roof over the run, propped up with stakes to keep it taut, although upturned plastic plant pots will need to be placed on top of each stake or they will eventually rub a hole in the mesh. Such a covering is recommended, as it will not only deter predators but also help to prevent the droppings of wild birds falling into the run and so reduce the risk of infection from bird flu (see page 118). An extremely effective way to reduce disease of a parasitic nature is to have two pens attached to the house. While one pen remains in use, the other can be rested, rotovated and reseeded to break parasite life cycles.

When building a gate to the run, make sure that the method used to fasten it is

secure. A central bolt often seems safe, but don't forget that a determined fox or dog pushing and scratching at the base of such a gate could force an entry. Instead, top and bottom latches are the better choice. The gateway must also be wide enough to allow for the passage of a wheelbarrow or any broody coops and runs that may be needed in the future.

Where different breeding pens of birds share the same dividing fence, it is imperative that some sort of screen is in place to prevent the cock birds from seeing each other. Without it, they will spend more time trying to fight one another than they will mating with their hens, and some serious injuries could also result. The easiest and least expensive way of forming this partition is by using one of the many windbreak materials sold by garden centres and horticultural suppliers. Sheets of corrugated metal are another, long-lasting option and, provided that they are painted to blend in with the surroundings, will not look obtrusive. If finances allow it or if you know of a low-cost source of planking, solid wood partitions can also be used, but they will need to be at least 60cm (2ft) high for bantams and twice that for large fowl.

If your birds are free range, electric netting can be used to create temporary runs as a means of protection. Electric poultry netting is made up of woven plastic string that is further interwoven with fine wire. The horizontal wires are electrified and the thick black strand at the base acts as an earth. A fencing unit provides the power and, as long as the vegetation at the base of the fence is kept trimmed or sprayed so that the fence does not short out, electric fencing is quite effective.

If you have a small permanent house with an integral run, a concrete base over which gravel, sand or bark chippings can be laid provides a hygienic base. Birds kept in such conditions will remain happy and healthy, so long as they are given a regular supply of greenstuffs in addition to their usual diet (see page 88).

Positioning the House and Run

Chickens can tolerate cold weather but dislike draughts; they love warmth but, having no sweat glands, are uncomfortable in extreme heat; and they delight in pecking through friable soil in search of insects but hate getting their wet feet. The ideal spot for a run therefore needs to be well drained and surrounded by some form of windbreak, and wherever possible the front of the hen-house should be positioned to face the morning sun but be protected from its hottest rays at lunchtime and in the early afternoon. At least part of the run should provide some shade at all times of the day.

Also bear in mind the run's location in relation to your own house and those of your neighbours, as even the best-maintained sites may encourage flies and a few unpleasant smells during the summer months. While you will enjoy watching the antics of your birds as they rush importantly about their business, your neighbours may not, so screening the run with trelliswork, hazel hurdles or other structures over which plants can be grown may well be appreciated. However, do be careful not to erect anything too close to the chicken run that could be used by predators as a means of gaining entry.

Do not site a permanent run on heavy ground with a high water table. If there is no alternative but to place it in a low-lying area, grade the site so that surface water runs away from the building. It is also a good idea to surround the house with

a 2m (6ft 6in) apron of gravel or walkway so that it does not become a mud-bath in winter. Fix guttering to large houses so that rain falling on the roof drains away, either into a water butt or a piped trench.

If possible, position the house as near as you can to any existing pathways so that the expense of creating new walkways is avoided. Large houses should be raised off the ground so that rats and other vermin cannot take up residence beneath them. The space under a raised house also has the advantage of providing extra room for your chickens and is an ideal place for them to dust.

Where chickens are confined to a wire run, they will soon make their own dust-bath, but a covered structure is very easy to build and will be much appreciated by the birds. All that is required is a small shelter consisting of four posts and a sloping roof about 1m (3ft) high. Turn the ground over inside the structure and leave the chickens to do the rest. You might like to add some fine soil, wood ash or sand to the mixture, but the most important thing is that the area remains dry.

Cleaning Routines

Inside the hen-house, it pays to gather droppings regularly – preferably each day but at least once a week. Make it part of your daily routine to remove the debris from the droppings boards below the perches and to replace this with a light covering of fresh wood shavings. If you leave the droppings too long, they will become hard and will be difficult to scrape off. About once a month in the summer and every two months in winter, nest-boxes need to be cleaned out and the bedding replaced.

In addition to the daily removal of droppings, all the floor litter in permanent houses must be removed at least once a year (preferably twice) and the interior

thoroughly disinfected. Try to pick a sunny day for this job and lock the birds out of the shed. Remove as many of the fixtures as possible, including perches, droppings boards and nest-boxes, and disinfect these and the interior with a virucide. A knapsack sprayer is more effective than a bucket and brush, as the higher pressure created ensures that the killing agents reach all the nooks and crannies where parasites love to hide. A steam-cleaning pressure washer is perhaps the best means of application; small units can be bought quite inexpensively.

At the same time as you disinfect the house, remove all covering litter from attached runs that have a concrete or compacted earth base. If you do not, there is a danger that parasites and bacteria could immediately be reintroduced to the house via the chickens' feet. If gravel, sand or bark chippings are used as the litter, it may be possible to rake or riddle the droppings and rubbish from the material, then disinfect it and re-use some of it, thereby cutting down on the cost of buying replacement litter.

Being smaller, movable fold units present a less daunting prospect when it comes to cleaning, so it is not too onerous a task to clear them out and disinfect them every six weeks or so. Even then, it is all too easy to let the six weeks become ten, so to avoid slippage keep a note of when the next 'service' is due, either on your kitchen calendar or in your book of poultry notes.

Feeders and drinkers should be kept clean at all times. Attach a small, stiff-bristled brush to your water bucket or watering can so that you can brush and rinse out the drinkers before refilling them with fresh water each morning – this takes no time at all. Feeders will not get too dirty if dry pellets or mash are used, but they will receive their share of droppings. As a result, you will need to clean them out as

a regular part of your daily routine. Every few weeks, drop both the drinkers and feeders into a proprietary cleaning solution and give them a thorough scrubbing.

Do not forget to give incubators, coops, brooders and other equipment not in daily use an annual spring clean. Incubators and brooders should preferably be fumigated both before and after use. You will find fumigation products at an agricultural stockist or advertised in poultry magazines.

Maintenance of the House and Run

As with most equipment, the regular maintenance of poultry houses and runs will ensure that they last for years. By replacing a loose board, re-stapling a piece of sagging wire netting, oiling hinges and regularly treating all exposed woodwork with a preservative, you can extend the life of these components almost indefinitely.

Obviously, any wood preservatives must not contain any chemical compounds that are likely to be harmful to the birds, so it is as well to read the instructions on the packaging carefully before making a purchase.

With the majority of modern products it is normally possible to treat the hen-house both inside and out, and then allow the chickens to return home just as soon as the wood is dry.

In addition to checking the hen-house itself, periodically inspect the perimeter of your runs for breaks in the fencing through which a predator could gain access. Although good-quality brands of chicken wire will last for up to 20 years, some inferior ones are made of lower-gauge wire and are not galvanized quite as thoroughly. It is a good idea to keep the fence free of vegetation so that any holes are more easily noticed.

Feeding
Chickens

You will get out of your chickens only what you put into them. If you feed them well and regularly, there is no reason why they should not produce eggs, meat for the table or a good crop of chicks. However, if they are not well fed, any nutrients they receive will be taken up with keeping their body functioning correctly. Fortunately, feeding your birds is simple and relatively inexpensive. They will find insects, seeds, grubs and fresh grass themselves in their run, especially if it is a fold type and can be moved regularly. To supplement this, they need two meals a day, the contents of which can be bought from any agricultural supplier or pet shop.

What Chickens Eat

Chickens are omnivores and, provided they are given the opportunity to do so, will feed on seeds, herbs and leaves, grubs, insects and even small mammals such as mice. All fowl are foragers, with an evolutionary instinct to range and search for food. They have excellent full-colour vision and a highly developed sense of hearing that, thousands of years ago, enabled them to keep track of the rest of the flock while ranging over vast areas of dense foliage in search of food. Even today's highly domesticated breeds have the same desire to hunt and, in the case of poultry, to scratch in their search for food.

Domestic chickens are typically fed commercially prepared feeds that include a protein source, vitamins, minerals and fibre. This usually takes the form of crumbs, pellets or mash, although generally all types of poultry (with certain exceptions, such as laying birds) also benefit from the addition of mixed corn to their diet.

Poultry have differing nutritional requirements depending on their age. Young chickens and bantams, for example, need much more in the way of protein when they are growing fast than when they are older and begin to grow more slowly – between, say, 10 and 18 weeks.

The Digestive System

Chickens have a very simple digestive system. Food is taken via the gullet (oesophagus) directly into the crop, where, by the end of the day, it will often show as a bulge in the chest, just above the breast and below the throat.

The food is softened in the crop – mash and pellets break down almost immediately, whereas it can take several hours for cereals to do the same. The food then passes through a glandular stomach

(proventriculus), which predigests it, and into the gizzard, where it is ground down by muscular action. As birds have no teeth, they would find it nearly impossible to make use of much of their food, especially wholegrains, without the aid of insoluble grit in their gizzard (see page 89).

Nutritional Requirements

Protein is needed by birds for growth, for tissue repair and for developing immunity against disease. Fats and carbohydrates are used to provide heat and energy, any surplus being stored in the body as fat, and fibre is required in small amounts to keep the bowels working. Finally, vitamins and minerals are needed to maintain health, while the latter are also used in bone and eggshell formation.

In the wild, a bird's food contains all the necessary fats, carbohydrates and plant and animal proteins it requires, plus sufficient levels of naturally occurring vitamins and minerals. However, as domesticated birds, chickens no longer have the freedom to make up their own nutritional package, so it is important that you offer them a diet that is well balanced, providing all their requirements at each stage of their life.

LEFT Scattering grain for the afternoon feed exercises the birds' foraging instinct and will keep them happily occupied for several hours.

Broody Hens

A broody hen eats very little when she is sitting, and requires little more than a simple diet of mixed corn, with plenty of maize to maintain body mass and warmth, along with fresh drinking water. No other specific nutrients are required. If fed grain she will also produce firmer droppings, making her less likely to foul her nest.

Chicks

Even if you have a home-produced or organic feeding programme in mind, do not be tempted to rear young chicks on household scraps. Without the correct protein levels at this stage, they are likely to die or, at best, will end up undernourished. Proprietary chick crumbs are essential, because they contain not only all the nutritional requirements, but also some necessary medicinal additives (to combat coccidiosis, for example – see page 119).

In most cases, chick crumbs can be phased out at around three or four weeks of age, but some inbred strains or more delicate true bantams may require crumbs for twice as long, as such chicks are often less efficient at absorbing all the necessary nutrients available in their food.

Growers

Proprietary growers' rations are the most sensible option for growing birds. They have a lower protein and vitamin content than chick foods. Pullets must not be overfed or given too much protein, or they will grow too quickly while still being immature internally. This will cause various egg-laying problems and possibly a partial moult at point-of-lay (see page 121).

Layers

Buy a good balanced layers' ration that provides around 17 per cent protein, and feed it either as a coarse-ground mash or as pellets. Grain or other low-protein foods should not be given with layers' feeds, as their addition will unbalance the manufacturer's carefully evolved formula, although in practice this appears to do little or no harm to the small, non-commercial flock.

Table Birds

If you are raising surplus cockerels for the table, household scraps can be an invaluable addition to their diet when combined with a high-protein proprietary fattening meal, and will certainly help in bulking them up. A bird fed in this way will have a great deal more taste than the majority of commercially produced chickens, and its varied diet (especially if maize is given) will make the carcass virtually self-basting. With this method of feeding, a bird is ready not after a certain number of weeks, but when it has put on enough bulk – pick it up, assess its weight and feel its breast. Cockerels as young as ten weeks can make magnificent eating; in the catering trade these are known as poussins and command a high price.

Breeding Birds

Birds that are used for breeding need a plentiful supply of protein and trace elements in their diet or their offspring may suffer from deficiency-related diseases. Breeders' rations are, as their name suggests, suitable for inclusion in the diet of birds you are intending to breed next year's stock from and should be fed from mid-winter onwards. Maintenance rations can also be fed to breeding birds, and in fact can be used during any period of a bird's life when its body is just ticking over, such as when it is in moult. Consider buying breeders' and maintenance rations produced for game birds, as these are some of the best feeds available.

Commercial Feeds

Assessing and combining all the required ingredients of a chicken's diet is a fine art, but fortunately there is no need to produce a perfect home-made mix now that balanced commercial foods are available. Anyone worried about unknown additives in commercial poultry foods can choose from free-range and organic rations that are free from such chemicals. Whatever your choice, buy high-quality foodstuffs from reputable firms.

Ornamental fowl pellets are available from some of the more specialist food suppliers. They are equally useful for bantams or large fowl, and are especially valuable if you want your birds to be in prime condition immediately prior to the show season. The pellets are also smaller than regular pellets, making them ideal for bantams.

Pellets or Mash?

While pellets may be the best option in terms of ease of use and reducing wastage, some experienced poultry keepers think dry mash is a better form of feed. Because birds can consume their entire day's ration of pellets in half an hour, they soon become bored, especially in winter. By contrast, it takes hens about three hours of continuous feeding to eat the equivalent amount of mash. If you are keeping birds for exhibition, however, pellets are your only option as mash is too messy – show birds, especially the bearded or muffed varieties, will end up with food-encrusted feathers around their beak if mash is used.

ABOVE AND LEFT When selecting feeding equipment, you need to allow at least 10cm (4in) of space per bird if you are using a trough and 2.5cm (1in) for a circular hopper.

Intensively reared chickens bought from commercial farms after their first season of egg-laying will almost certainly have been fed on mash. If you wish to change their diet, it is possible to wean them on to pellets and mixed grain. However, to build up their stamina when they first arrive, give them a warm mash mixed with such 'treats' as cooked vegetable peelings, cooked rice or crushed cornflakes. This will soon turn a poorly feathered, lacklustre hen into a blooming individual.

Where mash is being used, it is important to stir it well before feeding. Studies have found that mash ingredients such as ground limestone (included as a source of calcium) tend to sift through the food and settle at the bottom of the bag. Birds that are given food from the top of the bag may, therefore, miss out on some of these vital components.

If for any reason you wish to change the type of food you give, make sure you do so gradually, over a period of seven to ten days. Any change-over should roughly take the following pattern: mix in around a quarter volume of the new food to three-quarters of the old for two or three days; mix half and half for the same amount of time; give three-quarters of the new food mixed with a quarter of the old for another two or three days; then finally feed the new ration entirely.

Cereal Feeds

It is pointless trying to give a combined feed of pellets and cereal at the same time, as most birds will eat the wheat first and leave the rest. As cereal is harder to digest, it is best given on its own as the afternoon or early evening feed, thus ensuring that the birds go to roost with a full crop. The afternoon feed is also one occasion where an exception can be made to the rule of feeding chickens indoors. If

the corn is scattered around the outdoor run among dead leaves or any other suitable scratching material, they will gain a great deal of amusement and exercise.

The best mix for a cereal feed is wheat and maize, but the ratio should not be more than around one-quarter maize to three-quarters wheat. That said, a little more maize can be fed during the winter months, as it provides the ideal nutrients to allow the bird to maintain body heat. Too much maize in a laying bird's diet is bad for its health as fatty deposits can build up around the ovaries, but in table birds a diet high in maize will fatten them more quickly and give their flesh that 'corn-fed' colour. Split maize is a very useful tool in enhancing the colour of yellow-legged breeds intended for showing and its inclusion in their diet will often sharpen up faded legs. In addition, it improves the colour of egg yolks.

Bags of ready-mixed grain can be bought, but you may find that they contain barley, which chickens and bantams dislike and often reject in favour of other grains. It is therefore generally more effective, and less expensive, to buy wheat and mix in the maize yourself.

Sunflower seeds, linseed and other even smaller seeds intended for feeding to wild birds can be bought to help keep domestic poultry amused, although they should be given only as a treat rather than forming part of the daily cereal ration. It is more economical to buy such items in bulk rather than in the smaller bags sometimes seen in pet shops and supermarkets, but this is worthwhile only if you use them up before they reach their expiry date.

LEFT A mixture of wheat and whole or split maize makes a good afternoon feed.
RIGHT A few treats such as sultanas will be appreciated by your birds, and certainly help when taming new stock.

Never let your birds go without clean, fresh water. How much they drink in a day depends on the time of year, the type of food being given and the size of the bird. As with feed, you must be the best judge of how much your flock drinks, something that can be estimated only by careful observation on your part.

Household Scraps

If you are looking for maximum egg production, household scraps should not form more than 20 per cent of your hens' daily total food intake. If you are keen to utilize food scraps, you can boil them up and add them to mash, but make sure that the resultant mixture is moist but crumbly, not sloppy: if it breaks up easily when a mixing spoon is put through it, the texture is about right. Although this feed (called wet mash) is favoured by some poultry keepers, it is very time-consuming to prepare and you can put out only as much as the birds can eat in about half an hour or it will become sour and unpalatable.

Chickens enjoy any leftover stale brown bread (white bread is as unhealthy for poultry as it is for humans) soaked in milk, cheese, rice, pasta and any other cereal-based scraps. Do not feed strong-tasting, mouldy or otherwise contaminated food, as this will, at the very least, taint the eggs and, at worst, will cause digestive problems and even death. The discarded outer leaves of green vegetables can be given to chickens as part of their daily diet of greenstuffs.

Greenstuffs

Chickens need greenstuffs for the minerals and vitamins they contain, and in the case of free-range birds most of their requirements can be obtained naturally. In the early part of the year, grass that has been managed correctly will be high in chlorophyll, which, like split maize, is beneficial in improving the colour tone of yellow-legged chickens. Birds kept in runs or paddocks will also manage to find greenstuffs in the form of grass or weeds, but those in grassless runs will have to be fed a supply. A few turfs of short grass can be thrown into the run at intervals, but it is far better to hang fresh leaves off the ground or to put them in racks daily. Whatever method is chosen, any leftovers must be removed each night and placed on the compost heap. In addition to greenstuffs, windfall apples and any sweetcorn that has gone starchy and is too hard for use in the kitchen will also be readily devoured.

If you have space in your garden, you may consider growing crops especially for feeding to your poultry. Useful feeds include lucerne, vetches, green cereals, rape, kale, millet and clover. The birds will obviously also appreciate kitchen vegetables that have gone to seed. Always try to give them the whole plant, as they will benefit from the grubs and minerals in the soil surrounding the roots as well as from the leaves and stems.

Weeds gathered in the countryside, provided they are definitely free of agricultural or car-exhaust chemicals, can be another good addition to the diet. Young chicks in particular appreciate chopped dandelion leaves, plantains, shepherd's purse, watercress and, appropriately enough, chickweed.

BELOW A supply of mixed grit is essential for the chicken's digestive system.

Grit

Flint grit is essential in allowing birds to digest food once it has entered the gizzard (see page 83). Because stones on the ground are usually rounded, they have little effect on grinding food into the necessary consistency, so flint grit is given separately. It can be purchased from any agricultural supplier – expect each bird to consume approximately 30g (1oz) per month. Rather than putting the grit in a separate trough, some poultry fanciers place a thin layer in the nest-boxes in place of hay or straw so that the hens pick up all their necessary requirements when laying.

Grit is also a means of supplying calcium, and although this is often included in manufactured feedstuffs, it can be given separately as oyster shell or ground limestone. Many chicken keepers believe that birds fed good-quality layers' ration should not be given extra oyster shell because doing so will upset the calcium:phosphorous ratio and hence result in thin-shelled eggs, brittle bones and, in some cases, feather loss.

Vitamin and Mineral Supplements

While vitamin and mineral supplements are available commercially, they are not normally needed because the manufactured pellets and mash always contain the usual daily requirements. Birds that have access to grass will usually find sufficient minerals and vitamins as they scratch around, although there may be certain times during the year – such as in winter, when rearing birds and at the moult – when supplements may prove beneficial.

It is particularly important that sufficient vitamins are included in the diet of your breeding stock, otherwise the resulting chicks may hatch with curly, misshapen toes, splayed legs or twisted necks and breastbones. (It is important to note here that similar defects in incubator-hatched birds may, however, be a result of bad incubator management and have nothing to do with genetic deficiencies.)

When showing birds or moving them long distances, there is always a possibility that they might become affected by stress. This is another situation where supplementation is useful, as a course of soluble vitamins, obtained from your veterinary surgery and given in the drinking water for five to seven days, can help in alleviating stress. As sachets of soluble vitamins have a long shelf life,

they can usefully be kept on hand. Be sure to follow the vet's instructions to the letter and discard any medicated water that is more than 24 hours old.

When and How Much to Feed

The amount of food required depends on the breed of your birds, their stage of development, the time of year, and the methods and environment chosen to house them. Ideally, chickens prefer to feed shortly after descending from the roost and before laying their eggs. After some dusting and exploring, they will then quite often take a rest in the middle of the day, before feeding again in the mid- to late afternoon. If your feeding routine can reflect this, so much the better.

There are generally two options when it comes to feeding: ad lib and by hand. It is important not to overfeed your stock, as any surplus will encourage fat, unhealthy birds that will neither breed nor lay to the best of their ability, as well as the very real possibility of a plague of vermin. Most breeders prefer a programme of hand-feeding, as the correct quantities can be judged more accurately. However, where this is not possible (perhaps owing to commitments of work), you may have to compromise, with pellets or mash fed in a hopper in the morning and an evening scattering of grain. Remember that chickens are daytime-loving creatures, so the last feed should not be given so late that they have insufficient time to fill their crop for the long night ahead before going in to roost.

When estimating how much to feed by hand, work on the basis that a fully grown hen eats about 100g (4oz) of food a day, of which half (a good handful) should be grain. Particularly large breeds may require a little more – say, 150g (6oz). For adult bantams, a 60:40 ratio of pellets to grain

LEFT Drinkers are best placed outside the house to minimize wetting of the floor litter and prevent it being scratched into the water.

ABOVE Plastic feeders and drinkers are less durable than galvanized, but easier to clean.

is considered by many breeders to be a better mix, but it is up to you to observe their daily food intake carefully in order to determine the correct quantity. If you find no trace of food an hour or so after the birds have been given their breakfast, increase the amount until the last particles are being picked up around lunchtime. Conversely, if there is food left from the morning when you take out the afternoon grain supplement, decrease the breakfast quantity accordingly. Very young chicks should be fed four or five times a day, but once they are reasonably active and strong, a small trough or hopper can be used for ad lib feeding.

Food and Water Containers

When considering the size of feeder required, the important measurement is the outside edge: for a circular feeder, allow 2.5cm (1in) of the perimeter for each bird; and for a trough, increase this length to 10cm (4in) per bird. For reasons of biosecurity (see page 114) it is best to feed your birds indoors, but if you need to feed them outside from a hopper bought for the purpose, do not be tempted to buy one with a flat feeder pan. Feeder-pan bases must be conical so that the food flows into the trough freely and no unused or mouldy feed remains in the centre, something that would undoubtedly be the case with flat-plan models.

If you are feeding in the run or hen-house and are using troughs, these should be mounted on bricks or wall brackets so that they do not become contaminated with floor litter. For the same reason, circular feeders should be suspended from a cord or chain attached to a hook fixed to one of the roof beams.

Drinkers may be galvanized or plastic and come in several varieties. Allow 2.5cm (1in) of drinker perimeter per bird. Fountain drinkers are more hygienic on a day-to-day basis, but drinking troughs can be advantageous in the winter as the water they contain can be prevented from freezing over by floating glycerine on the surface each morning when you change it. For very small numbers of chickens or for bantams, earthenware dog bowls make good feeders and drinkers, as they are heavy enough to avoid overturning and are easy to keep clean.

Another option is to construct an automatic drinking system, which can be done quite easily by fitting a ballcock and valve into a heavy-duty plastic bowl. Water is supplied via an alkathene pipe fed from a mains water supply. It is important to check that the ballcock is working freely in order to prevent flooding, and to place the bowl on a level surface. Alternatively, low-pressure hanging drinkers can be obtained inexpensively and easily from any agricultural stockist. Suspend them from a tripod made of stout stakes or hung from a crossbar attached between two posts. Water is supplied from a header tank, not directly from the mains, and the filter that prevents sludge from fouling the spring-loaded release washer must be cleaned weekly. Both types of automatic drinker can be kept clean simply by turning them over and tipping the contents into a bucket so that the ground does not become soggy; they will then automatically refill and be flushed through.

Food Storage

The shed where you keep your chicken feed should be cool, dry and well ventilated, and the feed must also be protected from dirt, dust and vermin. Provided that the shed cannot be accessed by family pets, it is a good idea to keep several baiting points supplied continuously with rat and mouse poison.

Do not store feed bags directly on a stone or concrete floor, no matter how dry it appears, as condensation and moisture will undoubtedly build up between the floor and bag. This is the reason why agricultural merchants store their food on pallets or shelving

Do not use any manufactured rations that have gone past their expiry date. Not only is there a danger that such food will have gone off; any beneficial drugs or vitamins it contains will also be far less effective or even totally ineffective. If, for whatever reason, any food becomes damp or spoilt, discard it immediately.

If only relatively small quantities of food need to be stored, keep them in

ABOVE Dustbins make inexpensive vermin-proof containers for chicken feed.

containers that come complete with lids – galvanized ones are preferable, as rats can chew through even the most substantial plastic. Second-hand metal food-storage bins can often be picked up at local farm sales and auctions. Some of these even have dividing partitions, enabling you to keep pellets and grain in the same container.

All about Eggs

'What came first, the chicken or the egg?' This conundrum has puzzled humankind down the ages. Was it the hen, which after all lays the egg, or was it the egg, from which the hen hatches?

In the Beginning…

The Bible states that – along with other birds – the chicken was created, not the egg, but according to the theory of evolution, all new species develop from mutations. If the new characteristics generated through mutation turn out to be successful for survival, they are passed on to successive generations and a new species is formed. Genetic material does not change during an animal's lifetime, so the DNA of an embryo inside an egg is the same as that of the chicken it hatches into. The first chicken was a mutation of its avian parents, but its life began inside the egg, so it was the egg that came first – the remarkable, wholesome, miraculous egg.

And what an egg it is. Not only are chickens' eggs important emulsifiers used in all types of cooking, but they are one of the most nutritious foods money can buy. Even though they each contain just 307kJ (75 calories), eggs provide all the essential amino acids and minerals required by the human body, and are an important source of vitamins A, B and D. They also supply a complete protein that is of a higher quality than all other food proteins.

Hens fed a special diet containing 10–20 per cent flaxseed produce eggs enriched by the polyunsaturated essential fatty acid omega-3. This naturally occurring substance, commonly found in fish and fish oils, helps to lower blood triglyceride levels, promotes good vision and is required for normal growth and development in the human body.

Some people avoid eating eggs in the belief that the high cholesterol levels found in the yolk are harmful. It is thought, however, that egg yolk may actually lower total body levels of low-density lipoprotein, the undesirable form of cholesterol, while raising levels of high-density lipoprotein, or 'good cholesterol'.

Egg Formation

An average egg weighs 60g (2oz) and consists of three parts: the shell, which is made of calcite (a crystalline form of calcium carbonate); the albumen, or white, which is made up of water and protein; and the yolk, which is the most nutritionally valuable part of the egg.

Eggs develop in the ovary individually, then detach and slip into the oviduct, a long tube that ends in the vent, or cloaca, through which they exit the body (droppings are passed through the same orifice). As an egg travels through the oviduct, it rotates continually within the tube, the movement twisting structural fibres called chalazae into rope-like strands that anchor the yolk in the white from opposite ends of the egg. Once a fertile egg has been laid, the chalazae keep the germinal disc of the yolk on the uppermost surface, near the heat of incubation. This is why fertile eggs that have been transported must be given 24 hours to settle before incubation is attempted.

The hen's oviduct has two parts: in the first, the white forms around the yolk; and in the second, the shell is made and the pigment of the shell is deposited. Each egg takes 3–5 hours to pass through the first part of the oviduct and a total of 15–20 hours before it is ready to be laid.

While the colour of the shell has no relevance to the nutritional value of the egg, it is related to the ear or cheek colour of the hen (see page 12). Chickens' eggs range from snow-white to dark brown, covering all shades of beige in between, and some may be speckled and even blue or green (as produced by the South American Araucana breed).

The colour of the yolk is directly associated with the hen's diet. A very pale yolk can indicate that the hen lives in overcrowded quarters, is underfed or lacks

Eggs & Salmonella

The *Salmonella enteritidis* bacterium, which causes salmonella food poisoning, is found in the faeces of many animals, including chickens. Because hens sit on their eggs, there is a risk that the bacterium can enter the eggs through their porous shells. (Interestingly, it has been found that Maran eggs remain free from salmonella infection, possibly because the pores in their eggs are small and the bacteria cannot penetrate the shell.) Stringent cleaning and inspection procedures put in place since the 1970s have reduced the incidence of external egg contamination to virtually nil in commercial flocks, although *Salmonella enteritidis* can still enter eggs in the ovaries of hens before the shells have formed.

LEFT While commercially available eggs are almost invariably brown, keeping your own chickens means you can have the pleasure of collecting new-laid eggs in beautiful shades of chalky white, blue-green or olive.

Egg Games

Egg jarping, or egg tapping, is a traditional Easter game from the north of England and is rather like conkers. Players tap each other's uncooked eggs in turn until one breaks. The victor then goes on to the next round, until eventually there is only one good egg left – the winner.

•

Egg rolling takes place on Easter Monday, and again is particularly popular in the north of England. Hard-boiled eggs are rolled down a hill, and the winner is the person whose egg rolls the furthest, survives the most rolls or lands nearest a target, depending on the variation played. Easter egg rolls are also popular in the USA – the event on the lawn of the White House is the best known and has become an annual tradition. The first official White House Easter Egg Roll was held in 1878; today, the President and First Lady invite children from across the country to attend the celebration.

greenstuff, whereas a bird fed a diet rich in xanthophylls (the yellow pigment from the carotenoid group found in green leaves) will produce a darker yellow yolk.

Occasionally, a hen may lay an egg with no yolk at all or one with a double yolk. These are both the result of unsynchronized production cycles, and usually occur at the start or end of a laying period. The so-called 'meat spot' in the egg is, in fact, a small deposit of blood caused by the rupture of a blood vessel during its formation. It does not indicate a fertile egg. It is not harmful, but can easily be removed with the tip of a knife.

A cloudy white is a sign of freshness and is caused by carbon dioxide – this gas is present naturally in the white when the egg is laid, and decreases over time as it escapes through the porous shell.

Embryo Development

All birds will lay a clutch of eggs before starting to incubate them, and a hen is no different in this respect – she will just continue to lay as long as her eggs are removed daily and she thinks she hasn't produced enough for a clutch. The clutch must be complete before incubation starts, so each day the hen will add an egg and then leave it to cool. When enough eggs have been laid, she will go broody and will lose her breast feathers in order to warm the eggs and begin incubation. Her behaviour also changes: she will remain on the eggs, fluffing up her feathers and making croaking noises if approached, and will leave the nest only once a day to eat, drink and defecate.

The embryo of a large fowl normally develops inside the egg for 21 days, whereas that of a bantam has a slightly shorter incubation period (19–21 days). As it grows, its primary food source is the yolk.

It is important that the embryo doesn't become stuck on one side of the egg, so the broody hen will turn all her eggs several times a day. After 21 days, the chick pecks its way out of the shell with a horny growth on its beak known as the egg-tooth.

Once the chicks have hatched, the broody hen will remain on the nest for a further 24–48 hours. After this time, any eggs that have not hatched will be left behind when she takes her chicks on their first outing.

Certain breeds of chicken – in particular the Mediterranean varieties such as Leghorns and Minorcas – have had their broodiness bred out of them so that they produce more eggs. It is also rare for hybrids to go broody. As you may not always want to be hatching chicks, there are various methods of dissuading a hen from being broody. Sometimes, just isolating her away from the nest-box will do the trick. A more stubborn hen can be put in a cage with a wire bottom, so that the airflow cools her underside and discourages her from sitting, or you could try giving her a 'clutch' of ice cubes – although it may take several attempts before this cure proves effective.

Egg Storage

A fresh egg will keep quite safely for five to six weeks in a cool, dark, dry place. Always store eggs with the point down so that the yolk stays centred. As the shell is porous and will therefore absorb smells from its surroundings, eggs should also be kept away from strong-smelling foods such as fish or scented products like soap. The porosity also makes it unwise to wash eggs – if they are very dirty, brush or wipe them instead.

Many people keep their eggs in the refrigerator, but in fact they are better off in a cool place but not chilled. Refrigerated

Egg Sizes

Egg sizes in the UK now follow the European convention:

Small (S): less than 53g (1.9oz)
Medium (M): 53–63g (1.9–2.2oz)
Large (L): 63–73g (2.2–2.5oz)
Very large (XL): greater than 73g (2.5oz)

Egg-eating

Egg-eating is a habit chickens often acquire through simple curiosity. It starts when a thin- or soft-shelled egg is laid or a normal egg is broken and one of the birds in the flock pecks at it and decides it likes the contents. The bird will then do the same to any other eggs it may subsequently find.

Once egg-eating has become a habit, it can be very difficult to stop. Clean, dark nest-boxes will keep eggs out of sight and therefore reduce temptation. In addition, blown eggs filled with strong mustard can be put in the nest-boxes and may taste unpleasant enough to cure a bird, although you may have to do this for several days before the message gets through.

eggs frequently break when boiled, the absorption of bacteria through the porous shell is increased in the enclosed space, and the lower temperature can cause the protein to break down, reducing nutritional benefits. Take your cue from supermarkets and other food shops, which always store eggs on unrefrigerated shelves.

Raw eggs can be frozen very successfully and can be kept for up to a year. If frozen whole, the shells will crack, but the eggs can still be used for baking if defrosted carefully. A more successful way of freezing eggs is to put spare whites or yolks into ice-cube trays, defrosting the quantity you need as necessary. Cooked eggs do not freeze well, as they tend to be tough and rubbery when defrosted.

To tell if an uncracked egg is fresh, drop it into a bowl of water. If it sinks, it is fresh, but if it floats it is bad – bacteria have entered through the porous shell and have created gas inside. To tell if an uncracked egg is raw or hard-boiled, spin it, then abruptly stop it from spinning and immediately let go. If it starts to spin again, it is raw as the liquid inside will continue to rotate. If it remains still, it is hard-boiled.

Rules and Regulations

If you intend to keep large numbers of birds or plan to sell your eggs anywhere other than from your home, there are a number of regulations you must abide by. Some of these rules relate to food safety and egg traceability, while others are concerned with bird health.

In the UK, if you own more than 350 hens you must be registered with the Egg Marketing Inspectorate (this is free) and your eggs must bear a date stamp and your producer registration number to allow traceability. The stamp must be legible and applied with food-grade ink. The eggs must also be graded by size, which can be

done only at a registered packing station. If you own fewer than 350 hens but wish to sell your eggs, they must also be stamped with a producer registration number and you can only sell them ungraded. You do not have to mark eggs sold at your farm gate or delivered by hand to your customers, but they cannot be used in the catering industry.

Producer registration numbers are used throughout the European Union and look like this: 1UK 56789. The first number refers to the way the hens are reared: 1 = free range; 2 = barn reared; and 3 = caged. The letters refer to the country of origin, while the final five digits are unique to the producer.

If you keep more than 50 birds of any breed or species commercially in the UK, you must register them by law on the Great Britain Poultry Register. This is part of the programme set up by the Department for Environment, Food and Rural Affairs (Defra) to improve risk assessment and monitoring of bird flu outbreaks. Bird flu does not pose a danger to egg consumers, as the virus cannot survive cooking – in fact, often one of the first signs of the disease in a hen is that she stops laying.

To call your eggs organic, the layers must have access to an outside area all year round or be fed sprouted grains for any period they are kept indoors. All feed must be certified organic and cannot include meat by-products, and no antibiotics can be given. In the UK, eggs denoted as class A are the highest quality possible and may not be cracked, should have a normal shell and should not be washed – it is considered preferable to produce a clean, quality egg in the first place, as this indicates high standards of production. Class B eggs are of a lower quality and may be cracked or dirty.

Eggs in Folklore

There are many superstitions surrounding eggs. For instance, it was believed that the tenth egg laid in a batch would always be the largest, but to find a small egg was bad luck. Even unluckier was an egg with no yolk, as this was said to have been laid by a cockerel. Sailors were advised never to mention the word 'egg' if they were to avoid misfortune at sea. And anyone eating a boiled egg should always poke a hole through the bottom of the shell when they have finished to prevent a witch from using it as a boat, but shouldn't throw the shell on a fire or the hen will never lay again and a storm may brew at sea.

It is said that if a girl wants to find out who she will marry, she should boil an egg and then fast for a day. She should then take out the hard-boiled yolk and fill the hollow in the white with salt. While reciting an incantation to St Agnes, the girl must eat the salty egg, including the shell. The next man she sees will be the one she will marry – although if she takes a drink before sunrise, no matter how thirsty she becomes, her future husband's identity will not be revealed.

The first-century AD Roman historian Pliny the Elder wrote about a druid's egg, produced by the joint labour of several serpents and buoyed in the air by their hissing. Whoever possessed such an egg was sure to prevail in every contest and be courted by those in power.

'Columbus's egg' is the term used to mean a task that is easy once you know the trick. The story is that in reply to a suggestion that other explorers might have discovered America had he not done so, Christopher Columbus is said to have challenged the guests at a banquet given in his honour to make an egg stand on end. When none succeeded, he flattened one end of his egg by tapping it against the table and so stood it up, thus indicating that others might follow but that he had discovered the way.

Eggs Around the World

Thousand-year-old eggs are a highly prized Chinese delicacy, but despite their name they are, in fact, only around ten weeks old. The eggs are preserved in a coating of clay, ash, lime and salt, during which time the chemicals in the clay soak through the shell, turning the egg a translucent blue or green colour and producing a slightly fishy taste.

•

In Imperial Russia, giving eggs was not restricted to Easter. The practice was so popular that the Romanov royal family employed jeweller Carl Fabergé to create wonderfully ornate gem-encrusted eggs, to be given as presents at any celebration.

•

The word 'cockney' is thought to have derived from 'cock's egg', the name for the small malformed egg occasionally laid by a young hen. The term was applied by country folk to townsfolk generally, because of their reputed ignorance of country life and customs (cocks don't lay eggs), and in the 17th century specifically came to denote someone born within the sound of Bow bells – the bells of the Church of St Mary le Bow in the City of London.

Breeding
Chickens

As your enthusiasm for keeping poultry increases, there is bound to come a time when you will want to rear a few chicks, either just for fun or to replace ageing birds. Breeding from your own stock birds is the most satisfying option, but if you don't have a cockerel you can buy fertile eggs instead and hatch them under a broody hen. Borrowing a cock bird of proven pedigree and running it with your flock of hens for a month before returning it to its owner is another alternative. If you explain your plans to your neighbours beforehand, most will be prepared to put up with the crowing for such a short period of time.

Breeding Pens

Assuming that you own or can borrow a cock bird, he should be of the type described in 'Selecting a Breeding Cock' on page 29. For their part, the hens must be mature and should conform to the breed standard if there is one. Body size is important, and it should go without saying that all prospective breeding stock must be healthy.

The cock-to-hen ratio will depend on the breed; some males are virtually monogamous, while others are capable of fertilizing the eggs of ten or more hens. On average, however, one cock to six hens is about right, although you should seek the advice of an experienced breeder who has a good knowledge of your particular breed. If you want to produce birds for the table or for egg production, flock mating can be quite successful and involves running a number of males with selected groups of females at the rate of one cock to 10–15 hens, depending on the breed. Normally, however, single-male mating (not to be confused with single mating; see box on page 107) is practised.

If all your birds have been bought from the same breeder, there is a good chance that they will be related. As long as they are not too closely related, there should be no problem with this, but repeated inbreeding can result in undesirable traits in your strain (see box on page 107).

Cock birds can be run with the flock year-round, although professional breeders sometimes house them separately until the breeding season, believing that this keeps the males keen and eager to do their job. If the cock is kept separate, introduce him to the hens at least a month before fertile eggs are needed for hatching. Eggs may be fertilized within a week of mating, but it is best to allow a little more time to be sure. If a male of another bloodline is subsequently introduced, it is advisable to allow a fortnight after the changeover before beginning to save any eggs for hatching.

The Fertile Egg

If you have bought in fertile eggs, leave them for 24 hours so that the yolks can settle before incubation (see page 95). They do not need to be kept warm at this stage, as development will simply cease if the surrounding temperature is below 20°C (68°F). If the egg is then brought back up to a suitable temperature within a reasonable time period, either under a broody hen or in an incubator, the arrested development will resume and proceed as normal.

The length of time a fertile egg remains viable depends on the conditions in which it is stored. To obtain the best chances of hatchability, collect eggs as quickly as possible and store immediately at a cool temperature, as they will keep longer than those cooled more slowly through being left in the nest-boxes. The ideal storage temperature is 12.7°C (55°F). The storage time also depends on whether the egg will be hatched artificially or naturally with a broody hen. Generally speaking, eggs that will be hatched under a broody can be kept for around ten days, whereas those going into an incubator should not be more than a week old. It is interesting to note that chicks from eggs that have been stored are usually smaller than those from eggs that have not, and they also tend to hatch several hours later.

RIGHT Generally, the calm heavier breeds make the best broodies and mothers.

Broody Hens

You might notice that one of your hens stays in the nest-box longer than usual. If she remains there for a couple of days, put your hand under her; if she tries to peck at it, ruffles her feathers and squats further down into the nest, she is broody and is ready to hatch some eggs. However, before you give her fertile eggs to hatch, check that she is of a suitable type: most of the dual-purpose fowls sit well, as do cross-bred stock from heavy breeds.

The best location for a sitting box is in a shed well away from other birds. This should be well ventilated, fairly dark and free from rats – an old-fashioned coop and run is ideal. Cut a grass turf the same size as the box and place it upside-down in the bottom. This prevents eggs from rolling out when the rest of the nest is built up with hay, and it also helps to retain moisture and humidity, both of which are important for incubation. Do not move a broody hen from the hen-house to the sitting box in daylight; instead, wait until dusk. Make sure she is free of mites and lice (see pages 116–17), giving both her and the nest a good dust with flea powder before she settles down.

Rather than risking fertile eggs straight off, it is a good idea to put a dummy egg

RIGHT Only when a hen is sitting tight in her chosen nest should she be considered as a broody and given a clutch of eggs to hatch.

in the nest and then give the hen a day to acclimatize to her new surroundings. If, after 24 hours, she is sitting happily and tightly, encourage her out to feed and drink. You can then replace the dummy egg with a clutch of real ones. Just how many eggs to incubate will depend on the size of the hen, but it is often thought that an odd number should be set, as this makes it easier for her to turn them.

The broody should leave the nest once a day to feed and to empty her bowels. She may be so intent on carrying out her matronly duties that you have to lift her off – if this is the case, make sure you feel around her when you pick her up in case any eggs are tucked in her feathers. Keep an eye on her and do not let her stay away from the nest for more than 20 minutes.

Incubators

Hatching eggs in an incubator can be quite complicated and the results are nowhere near as successful as those you will achieve using a broody hen. There are, however, many small electric incubators on the market that may be worth experimenting with. If you are intending to rear poultry as a commercial sideline at some future date, an incubator will be essential – you cannot guarantee that broody hens will be around when you want them. Each incubator model is different, so it is important that you read and understand the manufacturer's instructions if you are to have any hope of success. If you want to hatch just a few eggs, a member of your local poultry club may be prepared to incubate them for you alongside his or her own eggs.

Although there are many incubator models, there are only two basic types: cabinet machines and those that work on a still-air principle. The latter are used widely and very successfully, have few working parts that can go wrong, are easy to understand, and are inexpensive and simple to maintain. Most of the modern models are electric, although you may still come across an older oil- or paraffin-heated version for sale at a farm auction. However, do ask someone experienced to check it over for you and make sure that all the essential working parts are present before you make your purchase.

Cabinet machines usually have more than one level of setting trays and differ from still-air models in that a fan circulates the air constantly to ensure an even temperature. Because of their size and capacity, they are normally used only by commercial chick producers. A separate hatcher is also required with a cabinet machine, to which the eggs are transferred a couple of days before they are due to emerge from the shell.

Humidity is an important aspect of incubator management, as an egg loses water through evaporation from the moment it is laid. During incubation, this rate of evaporation must be controlled by adding water according to the manufacturer's instructions. Too great a loss of water can cause the embryo to die, while too much can cause it to drown. Ventilation in the incubator is also crucial and serves two purposes: supplying oxygen and removing harmful gases such as carbon dioxide. Some machines have an arrangement of two or three felts, which are removed one by one at intervals of a week and let out the stale air.

Most modern incubators have fully automated turning devices, although you must check daily that the turner is working by noting the position of the trays or eggs. In older models, the eggs must be turned by hand at least twice a day to prevent the developing embryo from sticking to the side of the shell.

Common Breeding Methods

Line breeding uses two unrelated birds, the offspring of which are subsequently mated together in a systematic way to produce two distinct lines of chicken based on each of the parents. The lineage of any offspring, no matter what generation, are traceable to one or other of the original parent birds and, in theory, the gene pool of the first generation can be re-created endlessly.

•

Inbreeding is a method used to fix desirable genes, although it is not recommended for the novice as undesirable genes may also be passed on. The system is similar to line breeding, but brother–sister mating is used.

•

Outcrossing is when a totally unrelated bird is brought in to add new blood to an existing strain in situations where that strain has become weak through repeated line breeding or inbreeding. Like inbreeding, outcrossing can be risky, as unwanted traits may be introduced if the new bird has not been selected with the utmost care.

•

Single mating involves mating a single male to a single female and is uncommon except in the practically monogamous Asiatic breeds such as the Malay. It may also be the first step in a line-breeding strategy or as an outcross. (Double mating has a totally different meaning and is explained on page 29.)

ABOVE Candling is shown here in a commercial situation, but the basic principles are the same for the small-scale poultry breeder.

Candling

When an incubator is being used, it is advisable to check the eggs each week to ensure that the embryos within them are developing correctly. This is best achieved by candling, which involves holding each egg below eye level in front of a bright light, preferably in a darkened room.

Candling lamps can be bought or made inexpensively and consist of an electric light bulb placed inside a box, on top of which is an egg-shaped hole. The egg is held over the hole, such that no light escapes around its sides (most candlers have a rubber seal).

It is recommended that candling is carried out weekly to eliminate infertile, dead or damaged eggs. It is also a useful method for checking humidity by monitoring the air sac. At the first candling, at five to seven days, a fertile egg is indicated by the presence of the blood vessels of the embryo (these resemble a multi-legged spider), and the air sac should be evident at the broad end of the egg. As incubation progresses, the air sac becomes larger until, by hatching time, it takes up nearly a quarter of the egg, the remainder of which will appear almost completely blacked out. If the air sac is deemed to be too large at any stage, the humidity level inside the incubator must be raised. If the air sac is too small, lower the humidity, either by increasing ventilation or by reducing the surface area of any water trays in the incubator.

At 14 days, infertile eggs will appear clear and should be removed from the incubator to prevent possible contamination. This also improves the chances of the remainder hatching.

Candling and the whole process of incubation is too complicated to discuss in depth in a book of this nature, and it is therefore recommended that anyone interested in the subject reads the comprehensive, revealing and informative *New Incubation Book* by Dr A.F. Anderson Brown and G.E.S. Robbins (Blaine, WA: Hancock House Publishers, 2002).

Raising Chicks

Once the eggs begin to hatch, confine the broody hen to the nest-box and leave well alone. As soon as the hatch has finished and the chicks are dry, transfer them to a coop along with the hen. If the coop is in a shed, make sure that the hen cannot take her chicks too far from the nest by building a temporary pen. The sides of this must be tall enough to prevent her from flying over, otherwise the chicks will be left behind and may become chilled. If the chicks have been hatched in an outside coop, it should now have a run attached to it and be moved on to fresh, short grass. Feed the chicks on proprietary chick crumbs for the first three weeks and make sure their water container is shallow enough that they cannot drown.

If the chicks have been hatched in an incubator, it is possible to persuade a broody hen to become a foster mother to them. The hen must have been sitting on a clutch of dummy or even infertile eggs for at least a week and be well settled into the nest. Plan the arrival of the chicks for late evening and make sure that they can be kept warm for a couple of hours – buy a chick box for the purpose, or make one by placing a cloth-covered hot-water bottle in the bottom of a cardboard box. As dusk approaches, very gently take away a couple of the eggs under the hen and replace them with two or three chicks. The hen will not like being disturbed, and she

will fluff up her feathers and may even try to peck the back of your hand as you slide the chicks underneath her. Tuck them in among the remaining eggs, back off slowly and leave her to settle again. After an hour or so, if all is well, take away the remaining eggs and replace them with the other chicks. For maximum success the process must be carried out slowly and quietly.

Using an Artificial Brooder

If you do not have a broody hen to rear your incubator-hatched chicks, you will need an artificial brooder. This is usually located in the sectioned-off corner of a shed, with warmth provided by gas heaters or infrared lamps. If you have only half a dozen or so chicks, a conventional light bulb fixed in an upside-down terracotta plant pot will give off sufficient heat and the chicks will cluster happily around it.

Whatever heating system you choose, the room, shed or building must be maintained at a constant temperature, so forward planning is required. A metal roof, a sunny day and the heat from a lamp, for example, will obviously be a bad combination. Even with suitable surroundings, always keep a check on the ambient temperature inside the brooder, especially around midday.

Chicks need to learn where the source of heat is straight away. If rearing is carried out in a big shed, this is best achieved by making a circular surround of cardboard or hardboard and keeping the chicks within this. The heat lamp is then usually suspended from the ceiling at a height above the floor that ensures the temperature there is around 32°C (90°F). Each week the lamp's height is progressively increased until, by the third week, the temperature at floor level is down to 21°C (70°F). You can usually tell if you have got the temperature right by watching the chicks closely: if they are huddled under the heater, they are too cold; if they are seen pressing against the surround, they are too hot and the ring should either be enlarged or the heat lamp raised. After a few days, the cardboard surround can be increased to give the birds more space, eventually being removed altogether.

Once the chicks have reached the age of three weeks, the heat source can be turned off in the day during spells of warm weather. If only small numbers of chicks are being reared and the weather is hot, you could take the birds to a small wire pen on the grass outside for a few hours. However, make sure that the pen is cat-proof, situate it in the shade and take the chicks inside immediately should it start to rain.

Feeding Artificially Reared Chicks

Feeding and drinking vessels in artificial brooders should initially be placed around the heating area so that the chicks do not have to go far to look for them. Small jam jar-type drinkers are ideal, although commercial plastic chick drinkers are available. Chick feeders can also be bought, but almost any shallow pan will do provided that the birds aren't able to scratch their food all over the place.

Do not worry if you don't see the chicks eating during the first 24 hours as they still have enough nutritional reserves from the egg yolk. However, without a mother to show them what to do, you might have to encourage them to eat yourself by 'pecking' at the food with your finger. The inclusion of some finely chopped hard-boiled egg, sprinkled over the chick crumbs, will help to arouse their curiosity and also provides extra protein for the first couple of days. Do not mix up too much at any one time – as with wet mash for older birds, it will soon go sour.

RIGHT A Silkie or Silkie-cross bantam is considered by many to make the best broody.

Health
& Care

Good hygiene is essential to a bird's health, productivity and welfare, and is easily achieved by keeping accommodation clean, giving the birds plenty of room and feeding them a balanced diet. Sometimes, however, disease can occur in even the healthiest of chicken yards, usually brought in on the wind, via the droppings of wild birds that visit the pens in search of an easy feed, or even on the feet of human visitors. Maintaining biosecurity is, therefore, an important factor in ensuring the health of your stock.

Warning Signs

The best way to check the health of your birds is simply to sit and watch them for a time each day. Most chickens like to be part of the flock, so it is usually an indicator that all is not well if an individual is moping quietly in a corner on its own. The birds should always be busy scratching, dusting and feeding. Their combs should, in most breeds, be red and waxy and their eyes must always be bright. Drooping wings, ruffled feathers, a loss (or sudden gain) of appetite and loose droppings stuck to the feathers around the vent area should all be treated with great suspicion.

If the birds are tame enough, occasionally pick them up to check under their wings and in other downy areas for signs of fleas, lice and mites. At the same time, feel each bird's breast for any sudden loss of weight.

Biosecurity

Usage of the term 'biosecurity' has become more common since concerns over avian influenza (see page 118) have come to the fore. It is, however, really just a buzz-word for common-sense health measures. By periodically removing droppings from the run, feeding chickens in an area that is not accessible to wild birds and placing a disinfectant foot-bath at the gate to your poultry yard, you are actually carrying out most aspects of biosecurity recommended by government experts.

Handling Chickens

You will need to handle your chickens from time to time, to move them or to inspect them at closer quarters. First, however, you need to catch them. You may be able to do this by putting down some food and then quickly grabbing them by the legs, or you may be able to drive one bird into a corner and catch it that way. If all else fails, you will be able to catch them once they have gone in to roost for the night.

Birds should never be handled roughly as this will cause stress and may even damage them physically. To pick up a bird, place both hands over its wings, then lift and place it under your arm so that it is facing backwards. Keep hold of both legs with your hand and keep the wings firmly closed between your elbow and your body.

Minor Ailments and Conditions

If you do notice anything a little out of the ordinary, it is important not to panic. Your first approach should be to seek the advice of an experienced poultry keeper, preferably by getting him or her to visit, although a simple phone call may provide the reassurance you need. If you are still unsure about the diagnosis or treatment of an ailment, do not hesitate to contact your vet.

Colds

It is possible for chickens to catch colds, although the classic symptom of a runny nose may also be an indicator of other problems. As with humans, the likelihood of infection is increased by exposure to draughts, damp and sudden fluctuations in temperature. Colds will get better on their own, but it is possible to purchase avian cold cures from your vet or agricultural supplier.

Infectious coryza is a bacterial condition that produces symptoms similar to those of the common cold, including laboured breathing and swollen eyelids. Although this ailment is infectious, an antibiotic treatment is very effective.

Crop-Bound Birds

The crop of a chicken can become congested, or crop bound, for a variety of reasons, the most common being an obstruction caused by eating feathers, litter or long grass. Old-fashioned cures include giving the hen a drink of warm water to distend the crop, which should then be softened by rotating and massaging it by hand. If this does not work, a bird can sometimes be operated on, although in practice it is often necessary to destroy it and open up its crop for analysis. In this way, the problem can be identified and steps can be taken to prevent it from happening to any other birds in the flock.

Egg-Eating

See box on page 98.

Feather-Pecking

Typically, feather-pecking is the result of overcrowding and boredom. By giving your birds more space, dusting sites and a regular supply of greenstuffs, the habit can usually be eradicated, although once it takes hold it is sometimes difficult to stop. Very often, just one bird starts feather-pecking as a result of an inquisitive peck, and if blood is drawn she and others in the flock will be encouraged to continue. At the very least, the neck, rump and vent will be denuded of feathers, and at worst, the flock will continue pecking until the victim is so severely injured that she dies. Pecked birds can be sprayed with proprietary brands of anti-pecking remedies and the wounds treated with an aureomycin-based animal powder.

Fleas

Hen fleas are visible to the naked eye. Flea infestation in a bird is sometimes evident from weight loss and the appearance of bare patches in the feathers, and the comb and wattles may appear anaemic owing to blood loss caused by the feasting fleas. Fleas thrive in warm, humid conditions and are therefore more of a summer problem. Treat birds with a flea powder and spray all internal surfaces of the house in order to eradicate the flea eggs, pupae and larvae. A regular reapplication is recommended – as often as every three weeks in hot weather.

Lice

These parasites come in several different varieties, each of which has a preference for a certain area of the bird, but they are most commonly found around the vent area (and in the tufts of crested breeds). By parting the feathers, you may see small, light-coloured lice running between them. Look out for lice eggs in the form of a greyish-white encrustation around the vent and in the feathers under the wings.

Treat affected birds with either a liberal dousing of louse powder or a liquid chemical spray. A weekly dusting of nest-boxes will protect laying hens from becoming infested, but any cockerels will have to be treated individually.

Mites

There are several species of mite, the most common being the red mite. Despite its name, this parasite is, in fact, greyish-white in colour, becoming red only when it is full of blood after feeding on birds during the night. Red mites live and breed in crevices in the hen-house as near to their meal as possible – hence their fondness for the ends of perches and the interior of nest-boxes. Watch out for the characteristic signs of infestation – 'egg spotting', or blood spots from the squashed mites on the surface of eggs – and inspect the sleeping quarters regularly by torchlight.

Northern mites are similar in size to red mites but are grey or black in colour and live continuously on the bird's body, most often around the vent area. Birds suffering from a really heavy infestation tend also to become scabby around the facial parts. The red mite and northern mite can both be treated with a pyrethrum-based spray, although a single treatment is seldom effective and regular follow-ups are essential.

The scaly-leg mite differs from other mite species in that it affects only the legs and feet. Left untreated, the legs may become swollen and crusty, and eventually the bird will become very lame. The mite burrows under the scales on the legs, creating tunnels where it is able to breed. As it does so, the scales lift and distort. Old-fashioned remedies include sulphur ointment, paraffin and linseed oil. Petroleum jelly also works well, as it seals the gaps in the scales and prevents the mite from breathing, and vets recommend an application of gamma benzene hexachloride.

Prolapse

This condition is rarely seen in intensively reared birds but is quite common in otherwise healthy free-range birds. It occurs in immature or slightly overweight hens that have been laying heavily, and is caused by straining, the result being that the vent muscles are pushed out of the body with the egg still attached inside.

If prolapse occurs, the egg should gently be broken and removed, and the exposed organs then cleaned with a mild antiseptic. After this, they can be coated with a lubricant and pushed carefully back inside the abdominal cavity (this is more easily achieved if the bird is held head down). Keep the hen isolated in a small coop and run for a week, feeding her a diet of grain-based feed. Provided that the problem does not reoccur, the hen can then be returned to the flock.

Worms

Chickens are affected by two main types of worm: the tapeworm, which is flat and segmented; and the roundworm, which is round and smooth. The life cycle of each parasite usually involves a stage in the environment or in an intermediate host. Most, however, are passed from one bird to another by means of its droppings – fertilized worms are excreted and are then directly picked up by the other bird. Tapeworm eggs may also pass via the droppings or be retained within the rear segments of the worm, which periodically break off and are excreted. These eggs are then eaten by snails and beetles, which in turn are eaten by the poultry.

Birds suffering from a worm infestation may show an increase in their appetite combined with a decrease in egg production. Combs will look pink rather than red, and birds with a heavy infestation of roundworms will excrete bundles of dead worms. Preventative worming is normally carried out twice a year by the inclusion of a drug in the feed. Flubendazole is the most commonly used vermicide and can be prescribed by a veterinary surgeon, pharmacist or specialist agricultural merchant.

More Serious Illnesses

Any chickens showing obvious signs of serious ill health must be taken to the vet immediately, and any that die should undergo a post-mortem by a vet who specializes in poultry to determine the cause of death. Unless you are absolutely certain that you have made the correct diagnosis, do not attempt any treatment. While antibiotics are invaluable when used correctly, they should never be given as a standard treatment, as they may merely mask the true symptoms of a disease rather than cure it.

In the UK two diseases affecting chickens – avian influenza (bird flu) and Newcastle disease – are notifiable, which means that if you suspect an outbreak of either of these you must, by law, inform the Department for Environment, Food and Rural Affairs (Defra). It is advisable to keep abreast of any developments concerning these diseases, either through the media or, perhaps more reliably, via the statements periodically issued by interested organizations and the government's chief veterinary officers.

Acute Death Syndrome

The term 'flip-over syndrome' accurately describes this condition of acute heart failure. The causes of heart attack can be many and varied, and as a result they often remain unknown, but overfeeding is undoubtedly a contributing factor – the syndrome is not uncommon in commercially produced table birds prior to slaughter. If, in post-mortem examination, a fatty deposit is noticed around the heart, liver and kidneys, you have a legitimate reason to suspect overfeeding and should alter the diet of the rest of the flock accordingly.

Aspergillosis

This condition results from the inhalation of large numbers of fungal spores, which create lesions in the respiratory tract and cause obvious respiratory distress. Occasionally, an infection of the brain is also noticed in post-mortem examination. There is no treatment, so it is important to clean out damp feed, long cut grass and mouldy hay, straw or wood shavings from the run, all of which form the perfect mediums for the growth of the various fungi involved.

Avian Influenza (Bird Flu)

Bird flu has been given a separate section here owing to worldwide concern over the disease at the time of writing. The disease has actually been recognized since 1878, and by 1901 its cause had been identified as a virus and it was named 'fowl plague'. In 1955, its relationship to the mammalian influenza A viruses had been proven, but it was not until the 1970s that it was realized that vast pools of influenza A viruses also exist in the feral bird population. It is this latter fact that makes the control of any serious outbreak more difficult to put into effect, especially where poultry are kept outdoors.

The avian influenza virus, known as H5N1, breeds in the respiratory and intestinal tracts of infected birds and is transmitted from bird to bird, either by coughing and sneezing or through the faeces. There is currently little evidence of an airborne spread over long distances. The clinical signs are a cessation of egg-laying, a difficulty in breathing or, simply, sudden death.

Routine biosecurity precautions at home to prevent the spread of bird flu include keeping visitors away from your birds, ensuring that all feeding utensils in the hen-house are kept clean in order to reduce visits by wild birds, and the addition of vanodine or a similar product to the drinking water each day. Spraying the insides of the house on a weekly basis with a virucide will also help.

A vaccine containing an inactivated strain of the H5N2 strain is available against bird flu. The antibodies produced by birds given this vaccine are effective against H5N1 because the two strains are so similar. Although birds do need time to build up immunity following vaccination, tests have proven that transmission of the virus is halted after two weeks. The duration of protection is further increased by a booster vaccination given some six to ten weeks after the initial dose. Some countries have opted for a proactive policy of vaccination of domestic poultry, as this will help to avoid the need for millions of birds to be destroyed should a serious outbreak of bird flu ever occur. If you have any suspicions that your birds might be showing signs of bird flu, you must notify your vet or the appropriate government authority immediately.

Coccidiosis

Normally affecting only young stock, coccidiosis is bleeding within the intestinal walls and is caused by the coccidial protozoan organism. It is spread though droppings, so a good cleaning regime should ensure that the disease is not encountered. A natural immunity also tends to develop within a flock, and it has been found that young birds raised on wire floors, where they have no contact with their droppings, are more susceptible. Symptoms include a hunched appearance, ruffled feathers, blood in the droppings and/or sticky white diarrhoea coating the feathers of the vent area. Adult birds may lose weight and condition, bringing about a decrease in egg production.

Chick crumbs and growers' pellets contain anticoccidiostats that normally protect against the disease, although a vaccine is also available. Alternatively, it is possible to introduce coccidials to young birds at an early age so that they can build up a lifetime's immunity. If a problem occurs in untreated adult birds, your vet should be able to provide you with a prescribed drug.

Coronavirus

Several types of coronavirus cause disease in poultry, including infectious bronchitis, which results in respiratory problems and kidney damage. Generally speaking, the virus causing infectious bronchitis is airborne, spreads rapidly throughout a flock and can persist in an individual bird for several months. The first signs of infection are a drop in egg production and the appearance of rough, wrinkled shells on any eggs that are laid. It is possible to vaccinate against the various coronavirus diseases, and good biosecurity will help prevent their spread to neighbouring flocks.

Marek's Disease

There are several forms of this viral disease, a kind of herpes. The classic form appears as lameness in one leg, with the wing dragging on the ground. Some chickens will limp for a time then appear to recover completely, but this is, unfortunately, rare. Some breeds – such as Sebrights and Barnevelders – appear to be more susceptible, whereas Marans and Sumatras are hardly ever affected.

Stress is often the trigger, and pullets are particularly vulnerable at point-of-lay. A high incidence of parasitic worms and introducing the bird to a new environment can result in onset of the disease, which may hitherto have been dormant.

It is possible to vaccinate against Marek's disease, but obtaining small quantities of vaccine may be a problem for the average poultry keeper. An obvious answer is to buy birds that have already been vaccinated, or those that have been reared under a broody hen, as these seem to succumb to the disease only very rarely. Alternatively, consider clubbing together with other poultry keepers in a collective vaccination programme.

Newcastle Disease (NCD, or Fowl Pest)

Along with avian influenza, Newcastle disease is classed as 'notifiable' owing to its extremely infectious nature and potentially high mortality rates, although outbreaks can vary from very mild to highly acute. The disease produces various symptoms, including respiratory and nervous disorders, diarrhoea, lethargy and depression. In young birds, Newcastle disease can cause a severe reduction in growth and a number of secondary diseases.

It is spread by direct contact with secretions and excretions, especially faeces, and also via contaminated feed and water vessels. Because of the highly contagious nature of the disease, in some countries it is compulsory that birds are vaccinated before being allowed to enter any shows. As with Marek's disease, it might pay to form a combined vaccination group with other poultry keepers to reduce costs.

Bird Care

If you keep birds for exhibition, they will require some extra care in the days before a show to ensure that they are looking their best.

Washing Birds

Only birds that are to be exhibited are normally washed, and of these only the soft-feathered breeds. Washing hard-feathered varieties such as the Old English Game spoils the tightness of the feather conformation, so traditionalists 'polish' them with a silk handkerchief instead. Washing can also occasionally be necessary in breeds that have crests or feathered feet.

For showing purposes, washing should be carried out several days before the event so that the feathers have time to dry fully and hang properly. Most fanciers use two bowls of lukewarm water, the first ideally containing pure soapflakes, although washing-up liquid or baby or dog shampoo will do almost as well. Whatever soap is chosen, use only a little or it will strip too much of the natural oils from the feathers. The second bowl should contain clean water for rinsing, although the addition of some clothes whitener can be beneficial in the case of white or light-coloured breeds.

First, wash the feet and legs separately outside the main bowl, so that the dirt does not go into the clean water. A firm toothbrush or nailbrush is ideal for this, but any dirt that is ingrained under the scales can be picked out using a cocktail stick or a toothpick.

Next, holding the bird firmly so that it feels secure, immerse it in the first bowl of water and, starting at the head, very gently work the lather through the feathers in their direction of growth, taking care not to get soap in the bird's eyes. Once they have got over the initial panic of being placed in the water, most chickens seem to like this part and will crouch quietly in the bowl while they are being washed.

When the bird has been rinsed clean in the second bowl of water, pat it dry with kitchen roll or old towels; some exhibitors use a hairdryer, although if held too closely this can damage the feathers. The bird can then be left to dry completely in a box or poultry basket in a warm room or near a radiator. Once it is thoroughly dry, a show bird should then be put in a show pen in the penning room. If it is not intended for exhibition, the bird can be returned to the flock, although remember that the washing process will have removed some of the feathers' natural oils and so the bird may have less protection against inclement weather for a day or two.

Showing Tips

Every experienced poultry exhibitor has his or her own methods of enhancing a bird's appearance. For some this involves shaping and drying the feathers in a particular way after washing, while others may use rouge or baby oil to brighten a red comb, baby powder to whiten ear lobes or petroleum jelly to smarten up legs. There are a multitude of other tips that you will find out only by befriending a successful breeder, although he or she is unlikely to want to divulge any ingenious tricks of the trade if you are going to be in direct competition.

Finally, after a show, birds should always be quarantined for a few days before being returned to the flock to prevent the possible transmission of disease.

Anyone who is interested in showing chickens should read David Scrivener's comprehensive and informative book *Exhibition Poultry Keeping* (Crowood Press, 2005).

Moulting

Most birds shed their feathers annually in the late summer or early autumn, although young birds moult twice during their first six months of life. A partial moult sometimes also occurs in the early part of the year. This is often limited to the neck, especially in the case of point-of-lay pullets that have been given a layer's ration too early on in life.

If correctly cared for, a healthy young chicken will take around six weeks to change its feathers, whereas the process in older birds can take double this time. Some of the lighter breeds will also take less time than heavier, dual-purpose breeds. The large wing and tail feathers of all birds are replaced slowly in a specific sequence over an extended period of time. This sequence has evolved over thousands of years to ensure that birds do not lose too many feathers at once and so are always able to fly and escape from danger.

It is better for the bird if the moult takes place quickly, and in order for this to happen it must be in good condition. The later in the season a moult starts, the longer the whole process will take. And because egg-laying decreases or even ceases altogether in moulting birds, this means that a laying bird will remain unproductive for longer.

In order to get egg-laying breeds back into production as soon as possible, an early moult can be artificially induced by moving the birds into a different environment or by radically altering their diet. As soon as most of the hens in the flock are moulting, you can restore their usual feeding routine and give them an extra boost of linseed meal, soybean meal and cod-liver oil. Once they have produced their new feathers, increase the proportion of animal protein in their diet to encourage laying.

Killing Chickens

There will come a time when, because of illness, old age or taking a bird for the pot, it will be necessary to kill one of your flock. This is one of the least attractive aspects of the hobby and it may seem as if you are acting as jury, judge and hangman when making the decision to terminate the life of what may well have become a member of the family. Killing is, however, a necessity, and even though you may be able to ask someone experienced to do the job on the first couple of occasions, sooner or later you will have to learn to do it yourself.

Rather than unsettling the bird in question by chasing it around the hen-house or run during daylight, it is probably best if you can take it off the roost at dusk. Once you have caught it, remove it from the vicinity of its companions immediately. To ascertain whether or not a chicken is ready for the pot, feel for the two small pieces of cartilage on either side of the breastbone – these will tighten up with accumulated fat when a fowl has been properly fattened. By blowing or parting the breast feathers, the layers of fat can easily be seen, and the back should also feel fleshy and not bony to the touch.

The most widely used and, arguably, most acceptable and humane way of killing a bird is to wring its neck – although more correctly this involves dislocating its neck. For a right-handed person, it is most easily done by holding the bird's feet in your left hand so that it is hanging head down with the breast towards you and the back facing away. Next, grab the head with your right hand, so that the neck is between either your two middle fingers or your thumb and first finger, and the bird's head is in the palm of your hand. With a sharp movement, pull the head downwards and simultaneously rotate your wrist upwards, so the neck is stretched tight and the head is pulled back. You should feel the neck dislocate and may even hear a light crunch as the vertebrae break. Don't worry if the bird goes into violent spasms and flaps its wings for some seconds afterwards, as this is simply the nerves twitching in death.

Preparing a Bird for the Table

Birds that are intended for the table should be starved for 24 hours before killing, after which they need to be plucked, stubbed, have their head and feet removed, and be drawn (eviscerated).

Plucking

The plucking should be started at once. While the bird is still warm, remove the flight and main tail feathers. Then, sitting comfortably, hold the bird across your knees and start on the breast. Hold the skin tightly with one hand to prevent tearing, then with the other pull small groups of feathers out against the natural direction of their lie. Proceed in a similar manner over the whole body.

Any stubbly feathers (caused by new growth on a young bird) can be removed once the bird has cooled and the skin has begun to set firm. The bird should then be allowed to cool before the internal organs are removed.

Removing the head and feet

Turning the bird on to its breast, slit the skin vertically from the back of its head to its 'shoulder blades' and expose the back of the neck vertebrae. It should be possible to identify the break that occurred at killing by the presence of a small cavity of congealed blood; cut the head off at this point and, feeling with your knife, cut through the neck at its base where it connects to the body. You should then be left with the neck as a separate piece for your stockpot and, on the chicken carcass, a flap of skin folding over from the front.

Break and twist the legs at the rounded joint where the scaly part attaches to the thigh (you may need to cut around the joint with a knife if you do not have this action exactly right), and pull the feet away from the body. With a little physical effort they should come clean away, hopefully taking with them the sinews that run through the fleshy part of the thigh.

Drawing

The internal organs – some of which you may wish to keep for stock, including the heart, gizzard and liver – are removed by making a small incision between the vent and just below the parson's nose. Cut carefully around the rectum to detach it from the rest of the body. By inserting your hand into the gap created, you should then be able to remove all of the internal organs in one operation. Once you have pulled everything out, wipe the insides with a clean tea towel or several sheets of kitchen paper.

If you want to keep the heart, gizzard and liver, separate them from the rest of the organs, which can then be discarded. The gizzard is easily identified by its blue/silver colour and muscled appearance; its insides should be cleaned by cutting three-quarters of the way around its edges and opening it up like a book.

Finally, at the head end of the bird feel inside the flap of skin that was created by removing the neck and pull out the crop. Also, check that the windpipe (trachea) came away when the neck was detached.

Once prepared in this fashion, the bird is ready to cook, although there is no doubt that its flavour will improve if it is stored in a cool place for between 24 and 48 hours.

Crafts *with*
Eggs & Feathers

There is something deeply satisfying to the creator about home-produced goods, whether they are vegetables or art work, jam or clothing. In the chapter that follows are just a few ideas for making the most of your chickens. Once you get started you will find you are zealously picking up every feather they drop, saving empty eggshells and turning them into your own amazing creations.

The egg cosies are ideal presents for children to make and you can never have too many cards for birthdays or anniversaries. Everyone will be amazed to receive a pair of feather earrings, but be warned – egg painting can become addictive and all the family will want to join in.

Cress heads

Growing cress heads is a fun activity for all the family. For a different look use mustard seeds, which grow faster and produce slightly larger sprouts.

You will need

empty eggshells

•

waterproof ink or acrylic paint

•

paintbrush or pen

•

absorbent material (tissue, kitchen towel, cotton wool)

•

cress seeds

•

egg cups or acetate for bases

1. Wash out and dry the shell that is left over after someone has eaten a soft-boiled egg. Alternatively, carefully break a raw egg as near to the top as possible, tip out the contents, and wash and dry the shell.

2. Draw or paint a face on to the shell with waterproof ink or acrylic paints (a).

3. Fill the cavity to just below the top with the absorbent material and then wet it thoroughly with water. Sprinkle the cress seeds thickly on top and spray on a bit more water so that they are damp (b).

4. Balance your heads either in egg cups or acetate rings (made from sheets of acetate cut into strips and stapled into circles, like a napkin ring, to create stable bases), and put them in a sunny position such as a window ledge. Water daily.

5. After a few days the seeds will germinate, and after about a week your heads will have sprouted 'hair' (c). They will last for several days if you keep them watered and will grow a second head of 'hair' after they have been trimmed once.

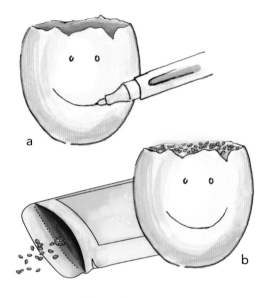

a

b

c

Felt egg cosy

Make a colourful chicken egg cosy either to keep your own breakfast egg warm or to give away as a present – perhaps with a box of your own eggs too.

You will need

tracing paper

•

squares of felt in your chosen colours

•

scissors

•

needle and thread

1. Trace the template on page 154 and cut out one of each shape A in your chosen colours of felt for the comb, beak and wattle. Cut out two shape Bs in the colour you have chosen for the main part of the cosy. Finally, cut out two shape Cs for the eyes, in a contrasting colour to the main part of the cosy (a).

2. Using the thread double (or strong fabric glue if you find the eyes a little fiddly to stitch), attach the eyes to the body shapes, making sure that the position of the second one is on the correct side (b).

3. Place the comb, beak and wattle (shapes A) between the two body pieces and sew the seams together, leaving the cosy open at the base (c).

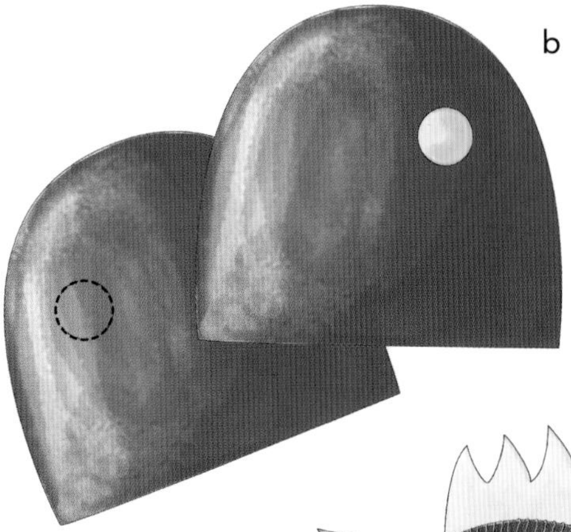

a

b

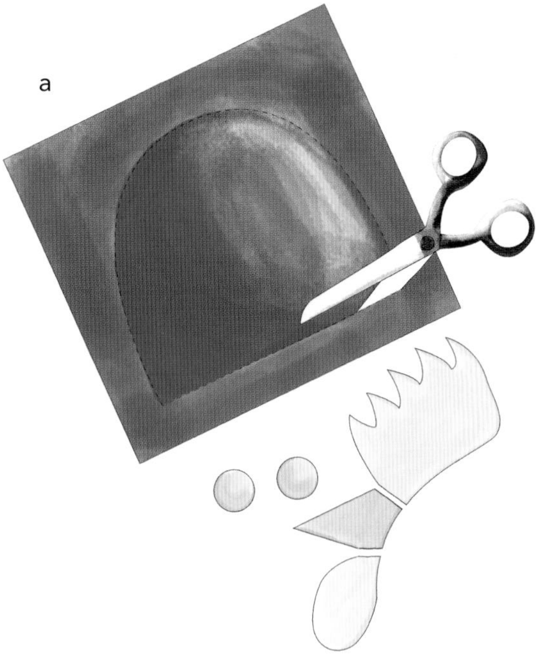

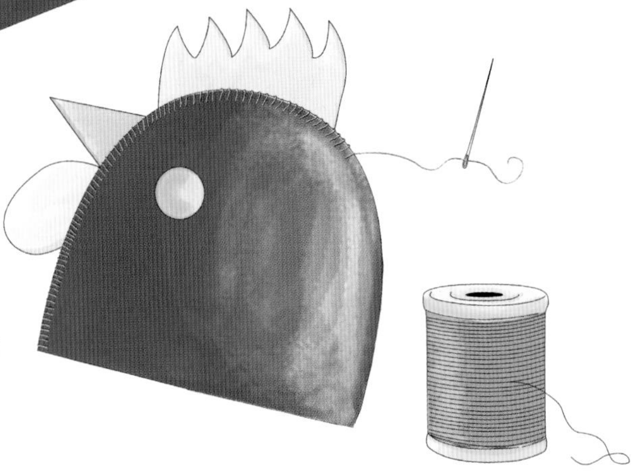

c

Decorated eggs

The tradition of decorating eggs at Easter dates back hundreds of years, during which time many different design techniques have been developed. Four contrasting methods are given on the following pages, along with instructions for the first stage – how to blow an egg. White eggs usually produce the best results when paint is involved, although attractively coloured brown eggs can also be used to good effect. To display your finished eggs, sit them in small rounds made from strips of clear acetate or in curtain rings, or put several together in a bowl.

You will need

fresh egg

•

sharp implement (compass, darning needle)

•

cocktail stick

•

syringe (optional)

Blowing an egg

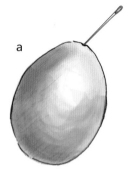

Before you can decorate your egg you need to blow it to remove its contents – if you do not, the egg will go off. Choose a nicely shaped egg, and wipe off any dirt on the outside before you start.

1. With a sharp implement such as a compass point or darning needle, pierce a small hole in the narrow end of the egg (a).
2. Pierce another hole at the wider end, making it a bit larger than the other hole while still keeping it as small as possible. Don't worry if it looks a bit messy, as this end won't be visible when you display your decorated egg.
3. Insert a cocktail stick through the larger hole and wiggle it about to break the yolk.
4. Holding the egg over a bowl (b), blow through the small hole. Although this is hard work, the egg should gradually come out. If you don't see any yolk, keep wiggling the cocktail stick – the yolk won't come out unless it is broken. If you really can't get any egg out you will have to enlarge the hole at the bottom. With practice, however, you will find that you can get the contents out through a remarkably small hole.
5. Try to get some water into the hollow shell through the larger hole (a syringe may help here) and shake it about to wash the inside, then blow this out and place the shell somewhere warm to dry out completely. The egg is now ready to be decorated.

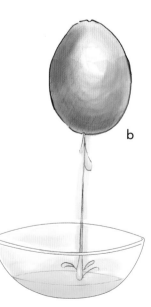

Découpage

No drawing or painting skills are required for this method of decorating your blown egg. You just need some patterned paper, glue and a pair of scissors.

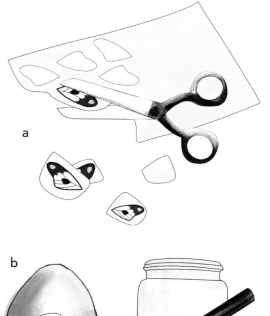
a

You will need
blown egg
•
patterned paper
•
scissors
•
PVA glue
•
varnish and brush

1. First choose your paper – look in magazines, use wrapping paper or specialist paper from craft shops, or experiment with transfers. Snip the paper into little pieces (a).

2. Simply stick these on to the egg with generous amounts of PVA glue (this dries clear) (b). If you can't mould a paper shape to the egg, snip slits in it and overlap them a little. Keep pressing the paper pieces on to the egg until it is completely covered.

3. When the egg is dry, give it two layers of varnish (c).

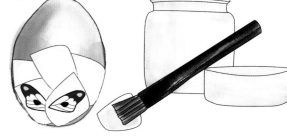
b

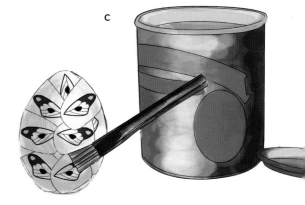
c

Sgraffito

This decorative method involves painting layers of colour on to a blown white egg and then scraping a pattern into this using a sharp point. A compass, darning needle (stick the blunt end in a cork, or you will find it hard to hold), craft knife or any other implement with a sharp, scratchy tip will do. When painting and varnishing your egg, balance it on a cocktail stick that has been stuck into an egg box so that it can dry evenly.

a

You will need
blown egg
•
Indian ink, acrylic ink or paint
•
paintbrush
•
white crayon
•
sharp instrument
•
varnish

1. Paint the whole egg with acrylic ink or paint.

2. Using a darker coloured acrylic or Indian ink, paint a shape such as a circle or oval on to the egg, or paint a strip around it (a). Allow this to dry thoroughly.

3. Using the white crayon, very lightly draw the important lines of your design on to the painted shape or strip (b) (you do not want the crayon lines to show on the finished piece).

4. With the sharp-pointed instrument, scratch out the design, removing the top layer of paint to reveal the coloured egg below (c). Scratch the outlines first and then add to them to create more detail. If you make a mistake or decide you don't like your design, simply paint over it and start again. With care, you can scratch through several layers of paint to create different colour effects.

5. Give your egg two layers of varnish – this is important, as it will strengthen the rather brittle shell (d).

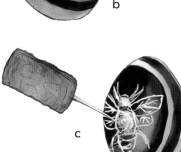

b

c

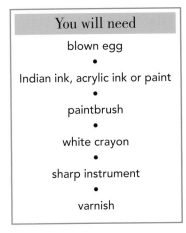

d

Chinese lacquer

For a Chinese design motif, look on furniture, soft furnishings or pieces of china, or get inspiration from magazines or books on antiques. Don't worry too much about the detail of the design you choose – a simple motif is often more effective.

a

You will need
blown egg
•
paintbrush
•
Indian ink, or black acrylic ink or paint
•
white crayon
•
liquid gold leaf
•
varnish

1. Paint your egg black with the ink or paint and leave to dry (a).
2. Very lightly draw your Chinese design on to the egg with white crayon (b).
3. Using the liquid gold leaf, paint in your design (c).
4. When the gold leaf has dried, coat the egg with two layers of varnish (d).

Variation Use maroon or celadon paint on a pale background in place of liquid gold leaf on a black base.

b

c

d

Spotty eggs

This very simple yet effective way of decorating eggs uses little round stickers, which are readily obtainable in packets from stationery shops.

You will need
blown egg
•
round stickers
•
paintbrush
•
metallic craft paint
•
varnish

1. Apply the stickers all over your egg (a).
2. Paint your egg with the metallic craft paint or any other type of paint you fancy, covering the stickers (b). Allow the paint to dry.
3. Peel off the stickers and colour in the white circles that remain in their place with a contrasting colour (c).
5. Give your egg two coats of varnish to strengthen it (d).

Variation Use another shape of sticker in place of the circles, such as stars.

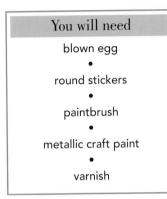

Feather printed cards

Card, envelopes and cellophane sleeves for packaging your finished designs, if you want to sell them, are all available in craft shops.

a

b

c

<table>
<tr><td>

You will need

newspaper

•

good quality card (250gsm)

•

black or coloured acrylic paint

•

paper plate, vinyl floor tile or any other disposable or washable flat surface for inking

•

paintbrush or paint roller

•

selection of feathers

</td></tr>
</table>

1. Spread newspaper all over your work surface, as this can be a messy operation.
2. Next, prepare your cards. Decide on the size you require and fold the card in half first so that you can position the feathers correctly when printing with them (a).
3. Squeeze some paint on to your paper plate or other inking surface, adding a drop or two of water if it seems too thick.
4. Take a feather and either roll or brush some paint on to its upper surface. Don't worry if the feather looks mangled – this will give character to your card (b).
5. Very carefully place the feather ink side down on to your piece of card (you may want to practise on scrap paper first). Cover the feather with a sheet of newspaper and carefully press all over with your hand (you could roll over the surface with a rolling pin or bottle, but the heel of a hand seems to work best).
6. Gently lift off the newspaper and feather, and admire your work (c). If you want to have more than one feather print on a card, do them one at a time, waiting for each to dry before applying another to avoid smudging.
7. Each feather will last for several prints, but you must throw the sheet of newspaper away every time to avoid getting in a mess.

Feather jewellery

Feathers make attractive and unusual jewellery that can range from the flamboyant to the quietly refined depending on your taste. At first the designs may seem rather fiddly to make, but with practice you will be able to produce your own creations relatively easily. Most craft shops stock beading wire, as well as jewellery findings such as ear hooks, necklace clasps, small rings and connections.

You will need

feathers

•

roll of 24-gauge beading wire

•

ear hooks

•

pliers

Feather Earrings

1. Select a single feather or a bunch of feathers and strip the fluffy part off the base of the central vein(s). If you are using larger feathers, strip them to the desired size.

2. Cut off 15cm (6in) of beading wire and thread one end through the eye of the ear hook. Keeping one end of the wire shorter than the other, bend the wire as shown in the illustration (a).

3. Holding the stalks of the feather(s) along the wire, wind the long end of the wire around the feather(s) once as tightly as you can (b). Fold the short end of the wire up as shown (c), then continue winding the long end around until it reaches halfway along the shank(s). Snip off the protruding bit of wire and feather stalk(s), and continue winding until you reach the eye. Snip off the winding wire and press in the end (d) .

4. Repeat the process for the other earring to make a pair, taking care that the feathers used match on each side.

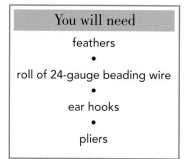

a

b

c

d

Variation To create a coordinating feather necklace, proceed in exactly the same way as for the earrings, but loop the wire over a chain, metal or leather-lace necklace.

Egg *Recipes*

Once your hens are comfortably housed, fed and watered, all that remains is to reap the rewards of your labours by collecting wonderful fresh eggs each day. The egg is one of nature's marvels – it binds, leavens, thickens and emulsifies, and is an essential ingredient in countless recipes, both sweet and savoury.

In spring you will find that you have more eggs than you can cope with, so the following recipes offer a few ideas for using and storing them. It is worth bearing in mind that very fresh eggs take a little longer to boil than week-old ones, are difficult to peel when hard-boiled and won't produce as much volume when whisked. In recipes where these qualities are important, such as meringues and pickled eggs, it therefore makes sense to use your oldest eggs.

Conversion Tables

OVEN TEMPERATURE

°C	°F	Gas mark	Oven heat
100	200	—	—
120	250	½	very cool
140	275	1	cool
160	325	3	warm
180	350	4	moderate
200	400	6	fairly hot
220	425	7	hot
240	475	9	very hot

WEIGHT

Metric	Imperial
10g	½oz
25g	1oz
50g	2oz
75g	3oz
100g	4oz
150g	5oz
175g	6oz
200g	7oz
225g	8oz
450g	1lb

CAPACITY

Metric	Imperial
50ml	2fl oz
150ml	5fl oz (¼ pint)
275ml	10fl oz (½ pint)
570ml	20fl oz (1 pint)
1 litre	1¾ pints

Note: do not combine metric and imperial measures in a recipe.

Baked eggs in mushroom flans

Serve this dish as a first course on its own or, with the addition of a salad, as a light lunch. It is equally good eaten cold as part of a picnic and will keep for several days in the refrigerator. These instructions are for six individual flans but you could use the same ingredients to make one large flan instead, using a 25cm (10in) flan dish.

Ingredients

225g (8oz) pack of ready-made
   shortcrust pastry
75g (3oz) butter
2 small red onions, finely
   chopped
2 cloves garlic, finely chopped
175g (6oz) exotic mushrooms
   (such as oyster
   mushrooms), chopped
175g (6oz) open-cap
   mushrooms, chopped
2 tsp lemon juice
1 tbsp fresh parsley, chopped
6 eggs
Parmesan cheese, grated

Preparation time: 25 minutes
Cooking time: 35 minutes
Serves 6

1. Preheat the oven to 200°C (400°F) and grease six 10cm (4in) individual flan tins.
2. Roll out the pastry and cut out six rounds to fit the individual flan tins. Press the rounds into the tins and put in the refrigerator to rest.
3. Melt a third of the butter in a frying-pan. Add the onions and garlic and fry gently until soft – about 15 minutes. Add the remaining butter to the pan and cook the mushrooms until their juices run, then add the lemon juice and parsley. Cook the mixture until all the liquid has evaporated, but be careful not to let the mushrooms burn.

3. While the filling is cooking, bake the pastry cases blind for 15–20 minutes in the preheated oven, then remove them and lower the temperature to 180°C (350°F).
4. Divide the filling between the flans, making a well in the centre of each with the back of a spoon. Break an egg into each hollow and sprinkle over a little Parmesan. Return to the oven and cook for 12–15 minutes until the eggs have just set. Serve immediately.

Pickled eggs

Traditional English pub food, pickled eggs are excellent eaten with cold meat or cheese and salad. Bantam eggs are ideal for pickling owing to their small size, and the longer you can leave them in the jar the better they will be. Below is a recipe for spiced vinegar, but you could replace this with any vinegar you like as long as the eggs are completely covered. The jars must have airtight lids.

Ingredients

For the spiced vinegar:
1.1 litres (2 pints) malt, wine or cider vinegar
25g (1oz) mixed pickling spice; or ½ tsp ground cloves, ½ tsp mace, ½ tsp allspice, ½ tsp ground cinnamon and ½ tsp ground ginger (or a slice or two of fresh root ginger)
a few peppercorns

12 eggs

Preparation time: 2 minutes
Cooking time: 8–10 minutes
Makes 1 jar of 12 eggs or
2 jars of 6 eggs

1. To make the pickling vinegar, simply combine all the ingredients in a bottle and keep for 6–7 weeks before using, giving it a shake occasionally. If you can't wait that long, bring the vinegar up to the boil with the spices, leave to cool and use immediately.
2. Hard-boil the eggs for 8–10 minutes, giving them an occasional stir to try to keep the yolk in the middle as they cook. Plunge them into cold water and, when cool, shell them and pack them into clean, dry jars. Pour over the vinegar to cover, seal and store in a cool, dark place for at least 2 weeks before eating.

Hollandaise sauce

Traditionally served with fish, hollandaise sauce also makes a delicious accompaniment to fresh asparagus. It is also the key ingredient in Eggs Benedict: muffins split horizontally and lightly toasted before adding crispy bacon and a poached egg topped with lashings of hollandaise sauce – perfect for weekend brunch.

Ingredients

6 tbsp white wine vinegar
a few black peppercorns
1 bay leaf
225g (8oz) butter
4 egg yolks

Preparation time: 4 minutes
Cooking time: 2 minutes
Makes about 275ml (½ pint)

1. Put the vinegar, peppercorns and bay leaf into a saucepan and boil until reduced to 1 tbsp – watch carefully, as this happens very quickly.
2. In another pan, heat the butter until it melts and comes to the boil.
3. Put the egg yolks into a food processor and, with the machine running, strain in the vinegar and then very slowly pour in the boiling butter. The sauce is ready when it is thick enough to coat the back of a spoon and should be lukewarm rather than hot.

Variation To make paloise sauce, start off with the basic hollandaise sauce and add 1 tbsp mint sauce and 1 tbsp chopped fresh mint. This accompaniment turns roast lamb into something really special.

Smoked salmon roulade

All your guests will be impressed when you place a slice of this roulade before them at a dinner party, but it is not difficult to prepare and never fails. It also makes an excellent cold lunch in the summer, and you can replace the filling with whatever is available. If cucumber is used, however, the dish must be eaten on the day it is made or it will turn soggy.

Ingredients

Parmesan cheese, grated
50g (2oz) fresh white
    breadcrumbs
175g (6oz) Gruyère or
    Cheddar cheese, grated
150ml (5fl oz) single cream
4 large eggs, separated
freshly grated black pepper

For the filling:
225g (8oz) smoked salmon
150ml (5fl oz) crème fraîche
1 cucumber, peeled,
    deseeded, salted and
    left to drain

Preparation time: 10 minutes
+ 5 minutes finishing
Cooking time: 15 minutes
Serves 6–8

1. Preheat the oven to 200°C (400°F). Line a large Swiss-roll tin or shallow roasting tin with greaseproof paper or non-stick baking parchment and sprinkle with a little grated Parmesan cheese.
2. Mix the breadcrumbs and Gruyère or Cheddar together in a mixing bowl, then stir in the egg yolks and cream. Season with pepper. If the mixture seems very stiff, add a couple of tablespoons of warm water.
3. In a separate bowl, whisk the egg whites until stiff. Using a large metal spoon, fold one spoonful of the beaten egg whites into the cheese mixture to loosen it, then carefully fold in the remainder.

4. Pour the roulade mixture into the prepared tin and bake in the centre of the oven for 10–15 minutes until risen and firm to the touch. Remove from the oven and lay a damp tea towel over the tin until the roulade is cold.
5. Sprinkle a sheet of greaseproof paper with grated Parmesan and turn the cheese roulade out on to the paper. Spread the surface with the crème fraîche. Rinse the cucumber, pat it dry and dice it finely, then chop the smoked salmon into bite-sized pieces and arrange both ingredients evenly on the crème fraîche. Finally, carefully roll up the roulade with the help of the greaseproof paper and transfer it to a serving plate.

Spinach and ricotta soufflés
with anchovy crème fraîche sauce

The accompanying anchovy sauce gives this unusual soufflé a bit of bite. Everything can be prepared in advance, until the point when the egg whites are whisked. This final stage must be done at the last minute, or the soufflé will not rise. Make sure everyone is seated at the table when you are ready to serve – the soufflés will start to sink if they are kept waiting too long.

Ingredients

Parmesan cheese, grated
4 large handfuls of baby
    spinach leaves
50g (2oz) butter, plus a little
    extra for greasing
50g (2oz) plain flour
275ml (½ pint) milk
50g (2oz) ricotta cheese
4 large eggs, separated
ground nutmeg, cayenne
    pepper, salt and black
    pepper to taste

For the sauce:
4 anchovy fillets
275ml (10fl oz) tub crème
    fraîche
squeeze of lemon juice
pinch of cayenne pepper

Preparation time: 30 minutes
Cooking time: 25–30 minutes
Serves 8

1. Preheat the oven to 190°C (375°F). Butter the insides of eight ramekins and dust them lightly with Parmesan.
2. Wash the spinach, put it in a large saucepan over a medium heat and cover with a lid. There should be no need to add more water, but be careful not to let the spinach burn. Cook it for 4–5 minutes until just soft. Drain the spinach thoroughly by putting it in a colander and pressing down to get as much of the moisture out as possible. Chop finely.
3. Melt the butter in a saucepan, add the flour to create a roux, and then stir in the milk gradually and cook until the sauce has thickened. Turn the heat down as low as possible and cook for a further 5 minutes.
4. Remove the sauce from the heat and transfer it to a large bowl. Beat in the chopped spinach, ricotta cheese and egg yolks, and season to taste.

5. In a separate bowl, beat the egg whites until stiff, then use a metal spoon to fold one spoonful into the spinach mixture to loosen it. Carefully fold the remaining egg whites in and divide the mixture equally among the eight ramekins. Wipe around the inside rim of the ramekins to give a neat finish, and sprinkle the surface of each soufflé with Parmesan. Bake for 25–30 minutes or until well risen and browned on top.
6. Meanwhile, to make the anchovy crème fraîche sauce, mash the anchovy fillets with a fork and fold into the crème fraîche with a good squeeze of lemon juice and a pinch of cayenne. Serve the sauce separately in a jug, or make a slit in the top of the soufflés and pour a little of the sauce into each.

Meringues

Meringues are a brilliant way of using up egg whites and keep beautifully for weeks in an airtight container. The quantity given here will make 12 individual meringues or one pavlova base. Pavlova always looks splendid: just cover the meringue base with whipped cream and pile on any fruits in season.

Ingredients
3 egg whites
175g (6oz) caster sugar

Preparation time: 10 minutes
Cooking time: 1 hour or
   overnight
Makes 12

1. Preheat the oven to 150°C (300°F) and line a baking tray with non-stick baking parchment.

2. Whisk the egg whites until they stand in soft peaks, then gradually whisk in the sugar until the mixture is stiff and shiny.

3. For individual meringues, use a metal dessert spoon to place spoonfuls of the mixture on the tray, making sure they are far enough apart so as not to touch as they spread during cooking. For a pavlova base, spoon the meringue mixture so that it forms a circle about 20cm (8in) in diameter.

4. Place the baking tray in the centre of the oven, turn the heat down immediately to 140°C (275°F) and cook the meringues or pavlova base for an hour. If you like your meringue dry, switch off the oven after the hour is up but leave the tray in there overnight.

Ratafia meringue roulade
with peaches

This very impressive pudding is actually remarkably easy to make. If peaches are not available, it is equally good with plums, or you could use raspberries and replace the ratafia biscuits with hazelnuts. Meringue freezes well, but do not freeze the whole roulade as the fruit may lose its juice when defrosted and turn the base soggy. The dessert will keep a day or so if you want to prepare it ahead of time.

Ingredients

5 egg whites
275g (10oz) caster sugar
100g (4oz) ratafia biscuits
4 large peaches
275ml (10fl oz) crème fraîche

Preparation time: 20 minutes
Cooking time: 27 minutes
Serves 6–8

1. Preheat the oven to 220°C (425°F). Line a 35 x 20cm (14 x 8in) Swiss-roll tin with non-stick baking parchment.
2. To make the meringue, follow step 2 in the previous recipe. Put the ratafia biscuits in a polythene bag and smash with a rolling pin. Carefully fold them into the meringue mixture, then pour it into the tin and smooth the surface.

3. Cook in the oven for about 12 minutes until golden, then lower the heat to 160°C (325°F) and bake for a further 15 minutes until firm to the touch.
4. Remove the meringue from the oven and turn it out on to a clean tea towel. Leave to cool for 10 minutes or so.
5. Drop the peaches into boiling water, then hold them under cold running water to peel them. Stone the fruits and chop them into 1cm (½in) dice.
6. Stir the chopped peaches into the crème fraîche and spread evenly over the meringue. With the help of the tea towel, roll up the roulade as tightly as possible. Don't worry if it cracks, as this is part of its charm.

Little chocolate pots

A treat for chocolate lovers. A little of this wicked pudding goes a long way so small servings are the order of the day. If you don't have ramekins, use little glasses or espresso cups, and eat it with teaspoons. The better the chocolate, the better the pudding. If you are having a party, make it a day ahead and keep the pots in the refrigerator overnight. Take them out at least half an hour before serving them.

Ingredients

6 egg yolks
325ml (12fl oz) double cream
275ml (10fl oz) milk
150g (5oz) milk chocolate
225g (8oz) dark chocolate
1 tbsp Tia Maria liqueur or strong black coffee
chocolate-coated coffee beans, orange zest or crystallized rose petals to garnish

Preparation and cooking time: 20 minutes
Setting time: 2 hours
Serves 6

1. Whisk together the egg yolks. Place the cream and milk in a saucepan and bring to the boil, then slowly whisk this into the egg yolks – it should thicken to a thin custard. Leave to cool.
2. Break the chocolate into pieces and place in a bowl set over a pan of boiling water (make sure the water doesn't touch the bowl) until melted. Whisk the custard into the chocolate bit by bit – it will thicken immediately – then whisk in the Tia Maria or black coffee.

3. Divide the mixture among six ramekins and chill. When set, decorate with chocolate-coated coffee beans, orange zest or, if you are feeling artistic, crystallized rose petals.

Lemon curd

Delicious spread on bread, lemon curd can also be used to fill small tarts or spread between the layers of a cake. It will keep for two or three weeks in the larder or longer in the refrigerator, but use plastic containers if you wish to freeze it, as glass jars may shatter.

Ingredients

225g (8oz) butter, at room
    temperature
450g (1lb) caster sugar
5 eggs
juice and finely grated rind of
    3 or 4 lemons

Preparation and cooking time:
15-25 minutes
Makes 3–4 jars

1. Cream together the butter and sugar in a bowl, then beat in the eggs one at a time. Slowly add the lemon juice and grated rind. Don't worry at this stage if it looks as if it has curdled – it hasn't!
2. Place the bowl over a saucepan of boiling water and, using a balloon whisk, gently whisk every now and then until the curd looks shiny and opaque, has stopped foaming and coats the back of a spoon – this may take anywhere from 10 to 20 minutes. Be careful not to let it boil as this may well cause it to curdle. Pour into sterilized jars.

Using up a Summer Glut

Most chicken keepers will at some time have an excess of eggs, usually in the summer months, and especially when the flock are fairly young. However many you give away to friends and neighbours, there may well be days when you are looking for inspiration on interesting ways to eat eggs.

Whole eggs

• Hard boiled eggs can be curried, stuffed, turned into Scotch eggs, added to kedgeree or salade niçoise.

• Poached eggs are delicious by themselves on toast, or you can add cheese sauce to create egg mornay, or sit them on spinach for oeuf Florentine.

• Oeuf en cocotte is simply an egg popped in a ramekin with a little cream and butter on top and baked in the oven.

• Omelettes come in all shapes and sizes – almost anything can be added but useful standbys are cheese, mushroom, tomato and ham. A variation is frittata or tortilla, which is basically an omelette that is not folded or turned. For a bit more bulk, add diced, cooked potato and onion.

• For something really special try scrambled egg and smoked salmon.

• Don't forget that old favourite, french toast (eggy bread) – a slice of bread soaked into beaten egg and fried till crisp and golden.

• Quiches, flans and soufflés – the sky's the limit here…

• A simple family pudding for using up eggs (and milk) is crème caramel.

Egg whites

Apart from meringues, egg whites are the basis of soufflés, mousses and sorbets. Apple snow is simply stewed apple with whisked egg white folded in.

Egg yolks

Zabaglione, mayonnaise (add garlic and you have aioli), custard, pancakes, crème brûlée. Some chocolate cakes and torte use frightening amounts of egg yolks – now would be the time to make one.

Glossary

Addled A fertile egg, the embryo of which has died during incubation.

Air sac The air space found at the broad end of the egg. It denotes freshness and, during incubation, the development of the embryo.

Auto-sexing Used of breeds in which the sex of day-old chicks can automatically be determined by the markings on their down. If the male of a black, red, brown or buff breed is mated to a barred or cuckoo female, all the cockerel chicks will have a white spot on their head and all the pullets will have plain black heads. This discovery led to the development of auto-sexing breeds in the 1930s. See also 'Sex linkage'.

Brassiness Discolouring in light-coloured breeds, caused by sunlight and weathering.

Brooder An artificial heater used for rearing young chicks.

Capon A castrated male chicken.

Debeaking Trimming back a bird's upper beak to prevent it from feather-pecking.

Droppings board A removable board fitted under the perches to collect faeces.

Dubbing The removal of the male bird's comb and wattles, first carried out during the days of cock-fighting to prevent injury. Until recently, show strains of some breeds – such as the Old English Game – were still dubbed, but the practice is now either illegal or frowned upon in most countries.

Ear lobes The patches of skin below a chicken's real ears. In most cases, the colour of ear lobes indicates eggshell colour: white-lobed birds lay white or cream eggs, while red-lobed birds lay brown or tinted eggs.

Frizzled Where each feather curls up so that its tip points towards the bird's head.

Gizzard A grinding stomach with a muscular lining.

Heavy breed A breed whose ancestry possibly derives from Chinese fowl.

Juvenile In relation to feathers, this is the first set of proper feathering to moult out before the adult feathers appear. In showing, a juvenile class category refers to the age of the exhibitor, not the age of the chicken.

Keel The bony ridge of the breastbone.

Light breed A breed that is usually Mediterranean in origin or has jungle fowl ancestry.

Meat spot A small deposit of blood in an egg, caused by the rupture of a blood vessel during formation.

Moult The period when a chicken sheds its old feathers and grows new ones.

Neck moult Moulting of the neck feathers only; it often occurs when a pullet starts laying before she is fully mature.

Oil sac A gland at the base of the tail that contains oils used in preening to keep the feathers in good condition.

Parson's nose The protruding lump of flesh normally covered by the tail feathers and seen only on a plucked carcass.

Primary feathers The long, stiff feathers at the outer tip of the wing.

Rust A show fault, denoting an undesirable reddish area on the wings of partridge, duckwing or pile-coloured females.

Secondary feathers The feathers on the outer side of the wing situated between the primaries and the point at which the wing joins the body.

Sex linkage When the sex of chicks can be distinguished at the time of hatching by their appearance. If, for example, a gold male is mated to silver females, the pullet chicks will follow the colour of the father while the cockerel chicks will be almost wholly silver.

Sickles Long, curved feathers on the outer side of a cock bird's tail.

Spur Pointed, horny projection at the base and rear of a cock bird's legs. Contrary to popular opinion, the length of the spurs is not a reliable indicator of a bird's age.

Strain A group or flock of chickens carefully bred over several generations by an individual fancier.

Trachea The windpipe, which forms part of the respiratory system.

Undercolour The colour of the fluff and lower parts of the feathers.

Variety A particular type of a pure breed – bantam Partridge and large Whites are, for example, both varieties of the Wyandotte breed.

Vent The orifice at the rear of a bird, also called the cloaca, through which droppings and eggs are passed.

Wing clipping When the primary and secondary feathers of one wing are clipped to unbalance a bird and so prevent it from flying.

Template

Felt egg cosy,
pages 128–129

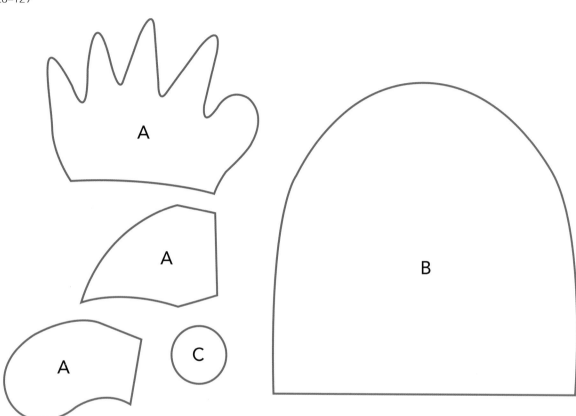

Picture credits

About the authors

Jeremy Hobson is a freelance writer living in France and is a member of the Association of Freelance Journalists. His interest in chickens and bantams began as a result of his grandfather's similar obsession. This was compounded when a friend of his father gave Jeremy a trio of White Wyandotte bantams, from which he developed his own strain and went on to win many major poultry prizes by the age of 15. Although the various varieties of Wyandotte bantams remain Jeremy's favourite, he has kept many other breeds during the ensuing 40 years.

Since 1983, Jeremy has contributed regularly to all the country-oriented magazines published in the UK and has written numerous books, including three for David & Charles. In addition, he has been involved with script-writing for BBC2 television and BBC Radio 4. Aside from poultry keeping, Jeremy's interests include all country sports, farming and gardening.

Celia Lewis studied life and portrait charcoal drawing with Signorina Simi in Florence. She has held various exhibitions in her home county of Surrey, England, and has had work shown at the Royal Society of Painters in Watercolour Exhibition at the Mall Galleries in London, where she won the 2005 RI Medal, as well as at the Royal Watercolour Society at Bankside.

Celia is also a glass engraver, producing sandblasted and drill-engraved pieces with a particular emphasis on natural objects such as butterflies, leaves and feathers. She finds her inspiration in her own garden, where she keeps chickens and guineafowl, and in the surrounding countryside, where she is a keen observer of nature.

Celia would like to thank Lily Blue of Godalming for the loan of decorative egg cups for the photography on page 101.

Index